T0147014

ON THE NATION AND THE 'JEWISH PEOPLE'

ERNEST RENAN (1823–1892) was a French philosopher, historian and writer. Among his many works were *The Life of Jesus*; *Antichrist*; *La Réforme intellectuelle et morale*; and the multivolume projects *The History of the Origins of Christianity* and *The History of the People of Israel*.

SHLOMO SAND teaches contemporary history at the University of Tel Aviv. His books include *The Invention of the Jewish People*; *L'Illusion du politique: Georges Sorel et le débat intellectuel 1900*; *Georges Sorel en son temps*; *Le XXe siècle à l'écran*; and *Les Mots et la terre: les intellectuels en Israël*.

ON THE NATION AND
THE 'JEWISH PEOPLE'

Shlomo Sand

Translated by David Fernbach

VERSO

London • New York

First published in English by Verso 2010
© Verso 2010
Translation © David Fernbach
First published as
De la nation et du «peuple juif»
© Les liens qui libèrent, Paris 2009

3 5 7 9 10 8 6 4 2

Verso
UK: 6 Meard Street, London W1F 0EG
USA: 388 Atlantic Ave, Brooklyn, NY 11217
www.versobooks.com

Verso is the imprint of New Left Books

ISBN-13: 978-1-84467-659-0 (hbk)
ISBN-13: 978-1-84467-462-6 (pbk)

British Library Cataloguing in Publication Data
A catalogue record for this book is available from the British Library

Library of Congress Cataloging-in-Publication Data
A catalog record for this book is available from the Library of Congress

Typeset in Fournier by Hewer Text UK Ltd, Edinburgh
Printed in the USA

Contents

Preface

Shlomo Sand

This little collection was originally designed for Israeli readers. None of Renan's writings had been translated into Hebrew, and I believed that my students were entitled to read him in the language they they knew. It is obvious why my first choice was the text 'What Is a Nation?', as this still has a great interest today thanks to its pertinence and its freshness. I then added the lecture on Judaism, which remains highly topical in relation both to Jewish history and to the dominant identities in Israel. I will not hide from the reader that the combination of these two texts was intended to reinforce certain 'scandalous' arguments that I put forward in my book *The Invention of the Jewish People*, as well as showing how far these were in some respects from being truly original. I was especially keen to show how, despite the fact that Renan questions the unity and nationality of the 'Jewish people', he was far from being anti-Semitic, any more so than this could be said of Marc Bloch or Raymond Aron.

The Unclassifiable Renan

Shlomo Sand

'Renan is certainly pleasing to read; but like the bee, he leaves a sting in the flesh' – Lucien Febvre, 'Renan retrouvé', 1949

In Edward Said's celebrated book *Orientalism*, Ernest Renan holds pride of place in the villains' gallery of historical figures. Said sinks his critical teeth into the copious body of texts of the French historian and philologist, extracting from these a welter of Orientalist quotations. Naturally, Renan is not the only individual incriminated in this brilliant essay: all the great luminaries of Europe from the start of the modern age offer a privileged target for Said's unrestrained anger. And yet Renan stands at the heart of the Palestinian-American's theoretical argument, and appears in a particularly dishonourable light.[1]

---

1   Cf. Edward W. Said, *Orientalism*, London 1978.

On the other hand, the wide-ranging essay on *Renan, la Bible et les juifs* by Maurice-Ruben Hayoun shows that, if acerbic and sometimes even mordant remarks about Judaism and the Jews are scattered across the works of the French philologist, Renan was, at the end of the day, neither racist nor anti-Semitic. Hayoun, a Jewish French philosopher, has immersed himself in the works of this nineteenth-century essayist and extracted a number of brilliant formulations and ideas, expressed both publicly and in private, that attest to Renan's admiration for the Jews and particularly for their success in ensuring their persistence in history.[2]

One might readily believe that Said's critique was a response to the sharp and tenacious arrogance that Renan displayed towards Islam and the Arabs – but that would be wrong. We might likewise cautiously assume that the laurels Hayoun bestows on Renan are explained by the warm and sympathetic attitude that Renan displayed towards Judaism and the Jews. As always, the truth between these two opposing approaches is not to be found in the middle – since no such epicentre exists. The major difficulty with any reading of Renan lies in the fact that his writings offer a good number of contradictions; even his most important works offer room for particularly varied interpretations. Besides, his ideas underwent radical and

---

2   Maurice-Ruben Hayoun, *Renan, la Bible et les juifs*, Paris 2008.

dramatic change in the course of his life, which Edward Said did not have the patience to examine, whereas Maurice-Ruben Hayoun, on the contrary, writes as an interpreter enthusiastic to produce a perfect defence.

A brief biographical reminder, designed to locate Renan's writings and the many ideas they contain in their specific historical time, can serve to clarify at least in part some of the ideological metamorphoses that occurred in the life of this great nineteenth-century French intellectual.

Joseph Ernest Renan was born in 1823 at Tréguier in Brittany, into a lower-middle-class family. Following the death of his father when he was five years old, his education and intellectual development was entrusted to his sister Henriette, who remained his companion throughout his life. He began his study at a Catholic seminary, where he was noted for his keen intellect and his inextinguishable thirst to advance and assimilate ever more in the way of culture and learning. His assiduousness impressed his teachers, and led to the invitation to continue his education in Paris, where he studied at the prestigious seminary of Saint-Sulpice. In parallel with his studies of theology, Renan acquired a deep knowledge of Hebrew and Aramaic, as well as of German philosophy. This later culminated in a remarkable doctoral thesis on the Islamic and Aristotelian philosopher Averroes.

Renan's studies, in the context of the cultural ferment of Paris in the 1840s, led to the first cracks in his religious sensibility, leading to doubt about his vocation for the priesthood. He definitively lost his faith and abandoned a career in the church. As he himself wrote, he then transferred his aspirations to a new vocation that was in the air at this time, that of science.

For a young scholar in the late 1840s, philology was the queen of the sciences.[3] Since the work of Friedrich August Wolf in the late eighteenth century, research into words and the relationships between them had been a prestigious discipline and was viewed as the most exact of the human sciences. Philology had also dealt a fatal blow to the age-old belief in the divine origin of language. For the former seminarian, theoretical linguistics became the decisive secular arm in the destruction of the religious myth that saw language as a gift from the Garden of Eden. It was now evident that communication through language was a human creation par excellence. So too was the view that the Holy Scriptures were the fruit of human imagination at a particular time. Renan's interest in religion never flagged; throughout his life this would be for him a subject of strong attachment and debate, but it would now be held in the firm grip of rational analysis.

The earlier Scripture appeared in Hebrew, a Semitic language par excellence, which Renan had mastered

---

3   See the chapter on philology in his book *L'Avenir de la science* [1890], Paris 1995, pp. 181–204.

perfectly, along with other languages of the ancient world. It was not by chance that his first major work was titled *Histoire générale et système comparé des langues sémitiques.*[4] Renan wrote this essay, which was awarded a prize by the Académie Française, at the age of twenty-four, the same year that he was appointed professor at the Lycée Vendôme. It was republished in 1855 with an addition and some modifications, and brought its author his first symbolic capital as a scholar.

Edward Said correctly identified this essay as one of the key ideological foundations in the crystallization of Eurocentric Orientalism, even as a work that conferred a 'scientific dimension' on racism at this early time. The mid nineteenth century was a distinctive phase in the 'dislike of the unlike' that is so commonly present in the history of the human race. After the ebb of the revolutionary wave of 1848, the 'springtime of nations', it was no longer Marx's spectre of revolutionary communism that haunted Europe, but rather scientistic racism.

In 1850, the Scotsman Robert Knox published his famous book on *The Races of Men.* Two years later there appeared in the United States James W. Redfield's essay *Comparative Physiognomy, or Resemblances between Men and Animals,* followed in 1853 by Carl Gustav Carus's

---

4   Paris 1855.

Symbolik der menschlichen Gestalt (*Symbolism of the Human Type*).[5]

In the same year of 1853, however, the most important literary event in terms of the arrogant claim made vis-à-vis the non-European Other was rather the appearance of the first two volumes of Joseph Arthur de Gobineau's *Essay on the Inequality of Human Races*.[6] This book rapidly became the bible of Europe's racist elite. Gobineau's two later volumes were published in 1855, the same year as Ernest Renan's *Histoire générale et système comparé des langues sémitiques*. The two authors were acquainted and exchanged letters, and they shared an identical approach and sensibility. Indeed, Renan's major philological work began with the remarkable admission:

> I am therefore the first to acknowledge that the Semitic race, compared with the Indo-European, does indeed represent an inferior combination of human nature. It has neither the high spirituality that only India and the Germanic peoples have known, nor the feeling for measure and perfect beauty that Greece has bequeathed to the neo-Latin nations, nor yet

---

5   Robert Knox, *The Races of Men*, London 1950; James W. Redfield, *Comparative Physiognomy, or Resemblances between Men and Animals*, Kila 2003; Carl Gustav Carus, *Symbolik der menschlichen Gestalt*, Hildesheim 1962.
6   Joseph Arthur de Gobineau, *The Inequality of Human Races*, New York 1998.

that deep and delicate sensibility that is the dominant feature of the Celtic peoples.[7]

This assertion seems to echo the position of the renowned German-Norwegian linguist Christian Lassen, who had maintained a few years earlier that the Indo-European personality was characterized by a breadth of vision and tolerance, whereas the Semite was egoistic and closed in on himself.

In the course of his book, however, a number of qualifications appear; Renan's writing was never simplistic or 'poetic', and was quite distinct from Gobineau's mode of expression marked by the seal of racist determinism. On many occasions, Renan's analysis displays a notable curiosity about certain Eastern cultures, and even an admiration for them.

It was likewise Renan's fundamentally anti-materialistic tendency that led him explicitly to reject the physiological distinctions made between Semites and Aryans: according to him, these two 'races' both belonged to the single bloc of the white 'race'. Yet behind his reservations, the caution and even distance he maintained in relation to Gobineau, a kind of biological essentialism continued to

---

7   Ernest Renan, *Histoire générale et système comparé des langues sémitiques*, pp. 4–5. See Renan's letter to Gobineau of 19 April 1854 in his *Correspondance générale*, vol. 3, Paris 2008, pp. 713–15.

illuminate the background of his linguistic ideas. Thus the final lines of his essay make clear to the reader the relative poverty of the Semitic tongues in relation to the Aryan, borne as they are by inferior human communities. Due in the main to their languages' lack of density, these communities are deprived of abstract thinking and the faculty of creating composite mythologies or sublime poetry. These comments, fixing the Orient in an inherent inferiority, would continue to echo in Renan's work for a good many years to come.

The 'scientific' guise in which a man of great learning could dress up the philological distinction between Semites and Indo-Europeans gave support and strength, among wide intellectual circles, to the popular biological distinction between Semites and Aryans that was increasingly widespread at this time. Against the background of Europe's industrial take-off and the increase in its economic gap with the rest of the world, as well as in an intellectual context where the evolutionary sciences, such as zoology, had become a model to be followed in the human sciences, Renan's 'scientific' hypotheses on the 'Oriental' mentality acquired the status of axioms. In the age of nascent Darwinism, their omnipresence in the discourse of the time is in no way surprising.

The success of Renan's book, and the publication at the same time of a collection of his essays, gave him a leading place among Orientalists. This led to his selection as leader of a French archaeological delegation sent to the Phoenician coast (present-day Lebanon) in order to organize excavations. The delegation went on to visit Syria and Palestine. This visit to the Holy Land gave a new stimulus to Renan's ever-keen curiosity about the difficult birth of Christian monotheism, leading him to write his *Life of Jesus*; even before its appearance, he was appointed to the chair of Hebrew at the Collège de France, thus reaching a summit of scientific prestige.

His inaugural lecture at the Collège de France in 1863, however, aroused one of the great storms with which the intellectual microcosm of Paris, 'capital of the nineteenth century', was so familiar at this time. The representation of Jesus as an ordinary human being, with all his particular attributes, provoked the indignation of the Catholic church, and enraged the battalions of clergy who enjoyed at this time the benevolent protection of the authorities. Under their insistent pressure, the unclassifiable Renan was suspended from his chair, to which he was restored only after the fall of the Empire in 1870. But if Renan was forced to relinquish this prestigious position, he acquired in return a media celebrity. His literary qualities, combining intelligence with the talent for popularization, made the *Life of Jesus* one of the first European 'bestsellers' in matters of theory. The book underwent several subsequent editions, and was acknowledged as a masterpiece by the leading scholars of the day.

Renan now became well known to a wide public, reaching far beyond intellectual and scientific circles. On two occasions he stood unsuccessfully for election to the Chambre des Députés as a liberal. But his political ambitions decidedly cooled in the wake of the French defeat in the war against Prussia, and the violent events that followed in connection with the Paris Commune. He succumbed to a phase of depressive torment about the future of his country.

France's military defeat turned Renan into an admirer of the Prussian monarchy, and he clearly expressed the deep despair that mass democracy aroused in him. He viewed the 1789 Revolution as a tragic mistake that had weakened and perverted France's development, and the country's future seemed to him uncertain.

German philosophy had always been close to Renan's heart, and this was now expressed in his adherence to a conservative, even reactionary, model, though as he no longer wanted to get his hands dirty, he kept his distance from any organized political activity and turned back to his old intellectual loves with renewed energy. In 1882 he completed his seven-volume work, *The History of the Origins of Christianity* (the *Life of Jesus* being the first part of this), and then worked, in the 1880s and through to his death in 1893, on writing a *Histoire du peuple d'Israël* in five volumes.[8] These two monumental works set

---

8   Ernest Renan, *History of the People of Israel*, London 1888–91. This multi-volume work ends with the emergence of Christianity.

the seal on his historiographical project, but did not mark the end of his intellectual development.

In the context of his renewed functions at the Collège de France (of which he had meanwhile become administrator), but also from other academic and public platforms, Renan delivered enthralling lectures that were immediately published as separate essays. These lectures, just like his many articles published in periodicals or newspapers, were the greatest evidence of his continual vitality, and confirmed his unchallenged status: he was certainly one of the thinkers who fashioned the hegemonic discourse in the French intellectual field.

It is fascinating to see how Renan displayed right to the end a curiosity attentive to the developing forms of political culture of his time, with no hesitation in confronting these. His liberal-conservatism definitively bowed before the logic of democracy, and he became one of the icons of the Third Republic.

In parallel with this, there began a significant retreat from the racialist conceptions that had haunted some of his writings. His advanced age did not prevent him from a rejuvenation of his arguments and from starting to reconceive the modern age.

From Ernest Renan to Ernest Gellner

'The nation is an imagined political community, and imagined as inherently limited and sovereign' – Benedict Anderson, *Imagined Communities*

The crystallization of the nation, guided by national ideology, is certainly a characteristic feature of modernity. Europe in the nineteenth century served as a great workshop for the creation of nation-states, progenitors and bearers of national mass cultures. And yet although the century was not short of original thinkers, very few of these were genuinely aware of the origin and nature of the changes underway in the politics of collective identity. The best of its philosophers and historians resembled Plato's cave-dwellers: immersed in the darkness of their cavern, they saw national shadows move on the wall of history, and believed that this was an eternal reality that had always existed. Ernest Renan can to a large extent be compared with the prisoner who has escaped from the cave, who manages despite the blinding light to identify the forms of animals and stars, and who on return to the cavern tries in vain to describe the reality of the outside world to the other prisoners chained up there.

On 11 March 1882, Renan was invited to deliver a lecture at the Sorbonne. To the surprise of his audience, he chose as his subject the question 'What Is a Nation?' The significance that he gave to the words pronounced on this occasion was hammered home by his preface to a subsequently published collection that included the text of this lecture:

> The piece in this volume to which I attach greatest importance, and to which I permit myself to draw the attention of the reader, is the lecture 'What Is a Nation?' I weighed each word of this with the greatest of care; it is my profession of faith as regards human affairs, and when modern civilization has collapsed in the wake of the disastrous ambiguity of the words 'nation', 'nationality' and 'race', I hope that these twenty pages will be remembered.[9]

They have indeed been remembered. Not in the course of the volcanic national eruptions that shook Europe in the first half of the twentieth century, but soon after. This text on the nation is incontestably the most cited among all of Renan's publications today. There is scarcely a single study of the idea of the nation that does not mention Renan's famous assertion that 'the existence of a nation is . . . a daily plebiscite'. His insistence on the voluntary and political dimension of collective modern identity was without doubt a novelty in 1882, and remained so for a century to come.

---

9   Ernest Renan, *Discours et conférences* [1887], Paris 1904, p. ii.

One can of course find in Renan's characterizations
aspects that are completely rooted in their time, alongside others that are far less so and represent an astonishing breakthrough. Renan's conceptual apparatus was
completely tied to the terminology of the nineteenth
century. 'Race' and 'community of blood' are expressions
that range freely among his polite and limpid sentences,
and though Renan sought to purge these of any political
context, they nevertheless attest to his essentialist starting
point. The term 'nation' still occasionally bears the mark
of his time, and is inadvertently used in unexpected places;
if Renan's 'nation' is a totally modern phenomenon, he
sometimes ascribes the adjective 'national' to notions of
the ancient world.

There is no doubt, however, that Renan stands far
and away above his contemporaries. At a time when the
Paris Société d'Anthropologie, a prestigious scientific
institution, collected African skulls in order to demonstrate European superiority, Renan opposed this dominant
tendency without the least ambiguity:

> Human history differs fundamentally from zoology.
> Race here is not everything, as with rodents or felines,
> and no one has the right to go round the world, fingering
> people's skulls and then seizing them by the throat and
> telling them: 'You have our blood, you belong to us!'

A similarly fascinating dualism can be found in the field of collective memory. Renan's approach remained notably positivist, and he saw national memory largely as a natural and spontaneous activity that developed according to its own dynamic. He did not perceive this, as he should have done, as the product of political and state undertakings. Renan delivered his lecture on the nation two years before the passage of the law on compulsory education, and of course long before the breakthrough made by Maurice Halbwachs in 1925.[10] The sociology of memory, which would much later analyse the modalities of the creation of remembrance, was still unknown to the learned author of 'What Is a Nation?', and his underlying conservatism also encouraged him to embrace the cult of common ancestors, whom he believed had to be remembered in order to make possible the sacrifice of victims to them today.

Yet despite this, Renan also displayed an uncommon originality in this dangerous field by pointing out that, in order to create a nation, it was necessary not only to remember but also to forget. He expressed in a particular way an underlying view of consciousness engaged with itself and involved in the processes of constructing the nation.

What then was a nation? As against a widespread belief, it was not an 'ethnic' body with a single origin. History had constantly mixed together groups of diverse origins

---

10   Maurice Halbwachs, *On Collective Memory*, Chicago 1992.

and created new societies. Drawing on history, culture and politics, Renan rejected any primordial approach that ascribed one particular group a privileged position in the field of defining the nation. Today's British, French, Germans, Italians and all others were mixtures who had come from different backgrounds, corresponding to various episodes of conquest, upheaval and migration. Nor were language, religion, geography or economic interest decisive starting points for national self-determination: there were nations without a common language, alongside others endowed with one. Some nations had a number of religious beliefs, without this being a problem. The world was too capricious, in all its forms, for political communities to be fixed in a single identity. National allegiance was not always a function of material needs.

In Renan's eyes, the nation was before all else a solidarity between modern and autonomous subjects, wishing to live under a single sovereignty. Why modern? Because the nation was a political idea created by people with free will.

This was clearly not on the same level as the important argument that Ernest Gellner would propose a hundred years later, to the effect that 'it is nationalism which engenders nations, and not the other way round'.[11] But of all the nineteenth-century thinkers, Renan is certainly the closest to those 'anti-primordial' theories of the nation that

---

11   Ernest Gellner, *Nations and Nationalism*, Oxford 1983, p. 55.

began to develop a century after his time. He was certainly the bearer of a national flame, and remained immersed in the mental mists of nineteenth-century romanticism; and yet his fundamental hypothesis, maintaining that nations are a historical construct specific to the modern age, with the implication that they will disappear one day and be transformed into new political creations, represented an impressive theoretical advance.

How was it possible for him to reach such a precursory point of view, while surrounded by nations still in a decisive phase of crystallization? Renan's 'genius', it would seem, was 90 per cent the result of an intellectual curiosity that was never assuaged, and 10 per cent the result of good fortune. The liberal Renan, who had throughout his life been embarrassed and perplexed by democracy, expressing reservations and even repugnance towards its mass effects, ended up accepting it as a historical necessity; and once converted, he remained faithful to it. And yet this unambiguous theoretical connection between 'democratic will' and 'nation as will' was to a certain degree the result of chance.

The annexation by Germany in 1871 of Alsace and a part of Lorraine aroused in France, as well as expressions of frustration and anger, intense and fascinating debates of principle. Already in 1870, Numa Fustel de Coulanges had questioned the German historian Theodor Mommsen over his support for the illegitimate occupation of conquered territories, affirming that 'it is neither race nor language that makes for nationality'.[12] This key phrase of the French historian, directed at his German colleague, became over the years the moral foundation for all opposition to the forcible annexation of these two provinces to the German Reich. The right to national self-determination was from now on welded to the right to democratic self-determination, and this contributed notably to restraining ethnocentrism in the definition of French identity. Renan also joined this debate, engaging in dialogue with his colleague and friend David Friedrich Strauss, the German theologian who had showed him the way in recording the life of Jesus. In an open letter published in 1870, when hostilities had ended, we can see the first signs appearing of Renan's steady opposition to identifying the nation as an 'anthropological' entity. Notwithstanding his admiration for the Prussian tradition, and his deep and persistent reticence towards mass democracy, he could not acquiesce in the forcible seizure of the two eastern provinces. After proposing in this letter a European federation as a way of resolving national conflicts, in a follow-up he explicitly mentioned the dangers that would lie in wait for Europe from an imperialist policy based on race.[13]

---

12   Numa Fustel de Coulanges, 'L'Alsace est-elle allemande ou française; réponse à M. Mommsen', Paris, 27 October 1870: http://www.bmlisieux.com/curiosa/alsace.htm.
13   See this correspondence in Laudyce Rétat, *Renan. Histoire et parole*, Paris 1984, pp. 639–55.

Other historical circumstances certainly played a role in Renan's feeling his way forward on the question of the inclusive or exclusive form of nationality, a question in which different French sensibilities came into play. From the Catholic tradition to the major linguistic differences still present in France, as well as the hegemonic ideology of the French Revolution, several factors oriented the politics of identity towards a conception of nationality that was less and less essentialist. But it was the annexation of Alsace and Lorraine above all that weighed in the balance and rendered the connection between nation and race, or nation and ethnic group, ever more questionable and impossible. Knowing how, in the modern world, the collective ownership of a national territory has a strength equal to the right of private property, all respectable nationalists had from now on to claim back territories that had been torn away from their native land.

It now became difficult, in fact, for authentic racists to base their national and territorial claims on biological assumptions. The populations of Alsace, as well as a good part of Lorraine, had too close a resemblance to their neighbours across the Rhine, all the more so as the greater part of them spoke a German dialect. In other words, from the 'ethnic' point of view they were too German. The appeal had therefore to be to the expression of their will. Moreover, their annexation to Germany had

been carried out by *force majeure*, without any consulta-
tion of the inhabitants of these regions, whereas, according to commonly accepted opinion, the majority of them
would have preferred, in the context of free elections, to
choose to remain part of France. It was on this anvil that
the national demand for the return of these 'orphan' provinces was forged.

The monarchist and Prussophile Renan of 1871 was
gradually transformed into a consistent republican and
patriot. To be sure, he did not extend to the populations
of the colonies conquered by France at this time the democratic principle of the right to self-determination that he
had adopted. And yet his reply to the question 'What is a
Nation?' amounted, from more than one point of view, to
a slap in the face for all those who sought to mix theoretical racism (still thriving in Parisian laboratories and other
research facilities) with political nationalism. From now
on, the far right would be reduced to seeking last-ditch
and confused syntheses between the idea of the nation and
Catholicism.

The tragic connection between 'scientific' doctrines of
blood on the one hand, and popular ethnocentric nationalism on the other, began to take firm shape precisely in
Germany. We cannot conclude from this that racism
disappeared from the public arena in France – the Dreyfus
affair teaches a sufficient lesson on this subject! And yet the
development of the 'Affair' and the balance of forces that

emerged in its wake show how Renan's theoretical initiative in 1882 linked up with a major underlying current that emerged in France and dominated the politics of identity, at least up to the occupation by Nazi Germany in June 1940.

We shall go on to see how a second major lecture that Renan gave a year later connects up with this inclusive current.

From Ernest Renan to Raymond Aron

'The Jews [are] a group of co-religionists originally brought together from every corner of the Mediterranean, Turco-Khazar and Slav worlds' – Marc Bloch, *Strange Defeat*

In January 1883, Renan was invited to deliver a lecture before the members of the Cercle Saint-Simon, made up of 'positivists' of various hues, including men of science and leading intellectuals whose declared objective was to spread French culture across the world. In the audience were some well-known racists and champions of colonialism, as well as intellectuals of Jewish origin.

The theme that Renan chose was not particularly surprising. He had completed his series of volumes devoted to Christianity, and his attention was now focused on his next major project, the formation of the first Western monotheism among the ancient 'children of

Israel'. But beyond the inherent interest of this research, his lecture was also motivated, it would seem, by a deep fear with regard to the emergence of a new Judeophobia on a supposedly 'scientific' basis. Four years before, the German journalist Wilhelm Marr had introduced the term 'anti-Semitism' into European terminology, raising the complaint that the German nation had been invaded by a branch of the Semitic race that had come from the east.[14] Hostility towards the ancestral religion thus received a scientific label and was transformed into a hatred based on empirical research: the Jews were Semites and thus foreign to the peoples of Europe, bearers of culture and progress. A few years later, with the appearance of the anti-Semitic leagues, 'science' was translated into politics and began to spill into the streets.

It is interesting in this context to note how the expression 'anti-Semitic prejudices' had already appeared in the 1860s, coined by Moritz Steinschneider, a Bohemian Orientalist of Jewish extraction, precisely in reaction to Renan's *Histoire générale et système comparé des langues sémitiques*. He was not the only scholar to reject totally the racist philological classifications that had been diffused from Paris and Berlin since the middle of the century. Likewise, Ignác Goldziher, a major specialist in Islam,

---

14   See Moshe Zimmermann, *Wilhelm Marr: The Patriarch of Antisemitism*, New York 1986.

and several other scholars of Jewish origin denounced the racialization of history of which Ernest Renan was then one of the pioneers.

The early 1880s, in fact, were a key moment in the history of this new hatred of the Jews. 1881 saw a great wave of pogroms strike the Jewish communities of the Russian Empire, affecting the whole of Eastern Europe. Renan joined forces with Victor Hugo in organizing a committee of support for the Russian Jews, and in 1882 protested publicly against the abject 'ritual murder' affair that had supposedly taken place in the Hungarian village of Tisza-Eszlar. We do not know exactly how far Renan was aware of his own indirect responsibility in the formulation of the new concept of race, now used above all in relation to the Jews. It is clear, however, that from the early 1880s he decided to mobilize fully in the attempt to dismantle the theoretical 'golem' that he had earlier done more than a little to manufacture. As was his custom, he invoked history along with an admixture of his personal impressions, sometimes rather naïve, in order to prove that the Jews were not a racial people but rather an integral component of the nations in which they lived.

Renan's lecture 'Judaism as Race and Religion' was essentially based on findings already well known to nineteenth-century historians: the population established in Judea, among whom Jewish monotheism emerged, had ceased to be an isolated ethnos, and had already developed and expanded by the adhesion of proselytes. If Israel had originally been an indigenous community (or, to use Renan's terminology, a 'race'), even before the rise of the Hasmonean kingdom it had undergone a shift towards a dynamic religion that actively converted tribes and peoples to Judaism. The desire to expand the community of believers was already notable in the Old Testament prophets (not that we have to accept Renan's dating of the Bible), and this desire formed a major aspect of ancient Judaism. By the Roman era, Jewish monotheism had converted several populations around the Mediterranean shores, and it continued this undertaking under the kingdom of Hadyab,[15] in the Arabian peninsular, in Ethiopia, and of course in the great Khazar kingdom of southern Russia. The world's Jewish populations were thus the result of proselytism, of enthusiastic religious propaganda work and the successful conversion of slaves and servants.

Renan particularly emphasizes, in a fascinating way, how the origin of the Jews of France was basically no different from that of Catholics or Protestants. 'We would probably find that the Gallic Jew . . . was most often simply a Gaul who practised the Jewish religion',

---

15   Hadyab (or Adiabene) was an ancient Mesopotamian kingdom that converted to Judaism in the first century CE.

he maintained, seeking to discredit the biological argument of the new Judeophobia that was rumbling around him. Jews were not unwelcome guests on French soil, but were there already before the invasion of the Frankish tribes. Renan reacts by means of opposition: there was not one Jewish type but several different ones. This was the result of historical processes: the isolation imposed in the ghettos and the prohibition of mixed marriages created the physical appearance that anti-Semites falsely ascribe to a race.

Just as the nation was not for him an ancient ethnos, but rather a mixture of linguistic and cultural groups, so Renan saw the practitioners of Judaism as an immanent part of the French nation.

Contemporary readers will very likely be surprised by Renan's thesis on the origin and history of the Jews across the world. After half a century of 'ethnocentric' historiography that seeks to preserve the specific character of Jews as a 'community of common origin', driven out of its homeland and scattered across the world, Renan's lecture is apt to disturb. We should bear in mind, however, that the hypotheses put forward by the French historian were not really original – neither in his own time, nor during the half-century after his death.

Around the same time as Renan delivered his lecture, Theodor Mommsen published the final part of his *Römische Geschichte*, in which he analysed the expansion of Judaism

in a manner very similar to Renan.[16] His colleague Emil
Schürer, often seen in the late nineteenth century as the
greatest specialist on the Second Temple period, was likewise of the view that the development of Judaism, in the
Greek world and the Roman Empire, could be explained
by large-scale preaching and conversion.[17] We should not
see it as an omission that the text of Renan's lecture, just
like the writings of all other historians, bears no mention of
the expulsion of the inhabitants of Judea after the destruction of the Second Temple or after the Bar-Kokhba revolt.
No study devoted to the 'exiling of the Jewish people' by
the Romans has been written, for the simple reason that no
such forcible expulsion ever took place.

The majority of French Jewish scholars received
Renan's lecture favourably, even though he attracted a
number of criticisms from other directions. This was not
only because of his essential conception of the Semitic
people, but also for his Hegelian view of the Jewish religion, which he presented as a monotheism that effectively
prepared the ground for the blossoming of Christianity.
But Renan's view of Judaism as a religion, not as the

---

16   Theodor Mommsen, *The History of Rome*, London 1996. Like
Renan, this eminent historian rejected the idea that the Jews constituted a racially defined people, and encouraged them to integrate into
the German nation. Cf. Theodor Mommsen, *Auch ein Wort über unser
Judenthum*, Berlin 1881.
17   Emil Schürer, *A History of the Jewish People in the Time of Jesus
Christ*, Edinburgh 1885, pp. 291–327.

racial identity of a people, along with his call to see Jews as French in the full sense, corresponded to the dominant state of mind at the time, both in terms of research and of politics, and so it remained for a long period.

The situation was unchanged sixty years later. In 1943, faced with the ravages of Nazism in Europe, the American Jewish Committee believed that Renan's lecture could be used as a major theoretical weapon in the struggle against racism and anti-Semitism. In the English translation of the text that appeared at this time, the final sentence of Renan's last work, the *History of the People of Israel*, was used as an epigraph: 'Israel will not be vanquished unless military force should once again take possession of the world, and found a new servitude, forced labour, feudalism. This is by no means probable.'[18]

The view that the Jews were essentially religious communities that thrived in various regions of the world – from the Berbers in North Africa through to the Khazars on the borders of Ukraine – continued to be accepted by the majority of historians in France and Europe until the 1960s. From Marc Bloch to Marcel Simon, many scholars who were of Jewish origin were inclined to believe that the majority of Jews in the world were descendants of

---

18　'Judaism: Race or Religion?', *Contemporary Jewish Record*, VI, 4, 1943, pp. 436. These 'prophetic' sentences can be found in Ernest Renan, *Histoire du peuple d'Israël*, vol. 5, Paris 1890, pp. 422–3.

converts. When Marc Bloch evoked his Jewish origin in one of his last writings, he saw it as logical to emphasize:

> I am, I hope, a sufficiently good historian to know that racial qualities are a myth, and that the whole notion of Race is an absurdity which becomes particularly flagrant when attempts are made to apply it, as in this particular case of the Jews, to a group of co-religionists originally brought together from every corner of the Mediterranean, Turco-Khazar, and Slav worlds.[19]

The secular and republican generation of Marc Bloch was well aware that the definition of Jews as a 'race' or a 'people' of unique extraction was a legend devoid of historical foundation, which frequently fuelled the anti-Semitic imagination. Scholars of the following generation likewise contested the very concept of a 'Jewish people', which had become a commonplace notion with the broad public. This was notably the case with the famous political philosopher Raymond Aron.

In 1983, i.e. exactly a century after Renan's lecture, Raymond Aron published his *Mémoires*, an impassioned work in which he offered personal reflections about his

---

19   Marc Bloch, *Strange Defeat*, London 1949, p. 3. For more on Marc Bloch and his relationship to Jewish identity, see the collection of his writings *L'Histoire, la Guerre, la Résistance*, Paris 2006, pp. 685–99.

identity, and about the utopias and myths he had always refused to accept. Notwithstanding his declared sympathy for the state of Israel, he did not hesitate to write, against the views of many others:

> What does the 'Jewish people' mean? Does it exist? Can we speak of the Jewish people as one speaks of the French people, or of the Basque people? The only valid reply seems to me to be that if one speaks of the 'Jewish people', one is using the notion of people in a sense that applies only to this particular case.

> Those who are called Jews are not, for the most part, biological descendants of the Semitic tribes whose beliefs and transfigured history are chronicled in the Bible. In the Mediterranean basin, just before or during the first century of the Christian era, there existed dispersed Jewish communities that had been converted to Judaism, not necessarily composed of emigrants from Palestine. Nor did all the Jews of Romanized Gaul come from Palestine.

> But these communities had none of the characteristics that ordinarily make up a people: neither a land, nor a language, nor a political organization. Their unity was based on their Book, their faith, and certain practices.[20]

---

20   Raymond Aron, *Memoirs*, New York 1990, p. 338.

As Raymond Aron saw it, it was the advent of Zionism, a phenomenon much closer to European nationalism than to the Jewish religion, that had transformed the age-old aspiration for a metaphysical redemption into a modern political demand. Nor did he hesitate to compare the Zionist myth, which posited a historical continuity stretching from King David to David Ben-Gurion, to the fascist myth that extolled the 'continuum' from Emperor Trajan to Benito Mussolini.

These positions, transmitted from Ernest Renan via Marc Bloch down to Raymond Aron, which stubbornly saw Judaism as a major system of belief rather than the identity of a people issuing from a common stock or a nation striving to regain its 'homeland', were a serious embarrassment to the Zionists. If Jews did not constitute a people and were devoid of a common 'popular culture', despite being the depository of an ancient religious culture, the modern champions of Zionism were obliged to nationalize this divine belief and integrate several components of Judaic religion into their national project.

Nevertheless, on the model of other inventors of nations across the world, the Zionists were not disposed to recognize that their 'past' was exclusively a religious one; they also undertook, in parallel, to construct retrospectively a 'Jewish people' that had been uprooted and exiled two thousand years before. In this way they counted on inscribing more certainly their right to the 'Promised Land'.

And so, whereas Moses Hess, one of the very first secular Zionists, eagerly imbibed the racial notions of the young Renan, the reaction to his lecture of 1883 by another major nationalist thinker, Moïse Leib Lilienblum, was among the most negative and condemnatory that it received. Lilienblum had been an adherent of Zionism well before Theodor Herzl, and was actually one of its founders. In the wake of the terrible wave of pogroms in Russia in the early 1880s, he was a leading figure in the Lovers of Zion, one of the first organized Zionist movements. In 1883 he published a virulent article against 'Renan's ravings', singling out in particular how the 'half-learned' Frenchman had dared to claim that 'the Jewish people, alive in our day, is not a seed issuing from ancient Israel, but rather a medley of inhabitants drawn from the peoples of Asia and Europe'.[21]

Renan's position went on to disturb several other Zionists. Some of these, in the line of Moses Hess, saw Jews as a racially defined people par excellence, while others distanced themselves from the purely biological aspect and were content with a more confused approach

---

21   Moïse Leib Lilienblum, *Autobiographical Writings* (in Hebrew), vol. 3, Jerusalem 1970, p. 27. See also Yaakov Shavit, 'An Intellectual Quartet: Muslims and Jews Reply to Renan', *European Review of Hebraic Studies*, IX, 2003, pp. 113–14 (in Hebrew).

basing itself on an 'ethnic community' that was slightly interbred, but remained none the less a sample of humanity the majority of whose members descended from a common origin. True, Zionist historians also acknowledged the conversions to Judaism around the Mediterranean, among the Berbers, and emphasized the role of the Khazars in a number of works down to the 1960s. But these historical accounts always necessarily included an 'ethnic' aspect aiming to demonstrate how, at the end of the day, the majority of Jews did indeed stem from 'Eretz Israel'.[22]

The process of decolonization across the Third World, the emergence of the Palestinian national movement and, parallel with this, the Israeli claim to Jerusalem – 'eternal capital of Israel' – after the 1967 war, contributed much to the growing refinement of this (non-linear) account of the origins, formation and expansion of Judaism in the world. The conquerors of the Holy City could not appear, not even in part, as descendants of Berber horsemen or Khazars. They had to be direct heirs of the warriors of the 'great kingdom' of David. Zionism had need more than ever of a solid ethnocentric legitimacy in order to justify the pursuit of the conquest of territory, and to have this legitimacy recognized by wide circles of Western opinion.

---

22   On this subject, see my book *The Invention of the Jewish People*, London 2010.

It was only logical, therefore, that the arguments of thinkers and scholars such as Ernest Renan, Theodor Mommsen, Marc Bloch or Raymond Aron, as well as a whole historiographic heritage, should become absolutely unacceptable. It is a bitter irony of history that, rather than continuing the lines of pluralistic research into this rich tradition, from the early 1970s the hunt was on, in Israeli laboratories of molecular biology, for marks of a DNA common to all the 'children of Israel'.

What Is a Nation?

Ernest Renan

Lecture given at the Sorbonne, 11 March 1882

I propose here to analyse in your presence an idea that is clear in appearance, but lends itself to the most dangerous misunderstandings. The forms of human society display the greatest variety. Great human agglomerations after the model of China, Egypt and the most ancient Babylon; the tribe, in the fashion of the Hebrews and Arabs; the city, in the fashion of Athens and Sparta; the assemblages of different lands in the manner of the Achaemenid Empire,[1] the Roman Empire and that of Charlemagne; communities without a homeland [*patrie*], held together by a religious bond, such as the Israelites and Parsees[2]; nations such as

---

1   The first of the Persian empires. The term 'Achaemenid' refers to the founding clan that won freedom from the Median kingdom around 556 BCE.
2   Followers of Zoroastrianism who left Persia in the wake of the Arab conquest in the sixth to seventh century.

France, England and the majority of modern independent European states; confederations on the pattern of the Swiss or American; affinities such as those which race, or rather language, established between the different branches of the Germanic or Slavic peoples – these are all modes of grouping that exist, or certainly have existed, and they cannot be confused with one another without most serious consequences. At the time of the French Revolution, it was believed that the institutions of small independent cities, such as Sparta or Rome, could be applied to our great nations of thirty or forty million souls. In our day, a still more serious mistake is made: race is confused with nation, and ethnographic or rather linguistic groups are ascribed a sovereignty analogous to that of peoples that actually exist. Let us seek to reach a degree of precision on these difficult questions, in which the slightest confusion over the meaning of words, at the start of the argument, can produce at the end the most damaging errors. What we shall do here is delicate, almost like vivisection. We shall treat the living much as one usually treats the dead. We shall handle them with the most absolute coldness and impartiality.

I

Ever since the end of the Roman Empire, or better, since the break-up of the empire of Charlemagne, Western

Europe appears to us as divided into nations, some of which, at certain times, have sought to exercise hegemony over others, without ever succeeding to do so in a permanent fashion. What Charles V, Louis XIV and Napoleon all failed to do will probably not be possible in the future either. The division of Europe is too great for an attempt at universal domination not to provoke very quickly a coalition that drives such an ambitious nation back to its natural boundaries. A kind of long-term equilibrium has been established. France, England, Germany and Russia will still be in centuries to come, despite the vicissitudes they may experience, historic individualities, essential pieces of a chessboard whose squares constantly vary in importance and size, but never completely merge.

Nations, understood in this manner, are something fairly new in history. They were unknown to antiquity; Egypt, China and ancient Chaldea were not nations in any sense. They were flocks led by a son of the Sun, or a son of Heaven. There were no Egyptian citizens, any more than there were Chinese ones. Classical antiquity had municipal republics and kingdoms, confederations of local republics, empires; but it scarcely had the nation in the sense in which we understand this. Athens, Sparta, Sidon and Tyre were small centres marked by an admirable patriotism, but cities with a relatively restricted territory. Gaul, Spain and Italy, before their absorption into the Roman Empire, were collections of tribes, often in alliance with one another, but without central institutions or dynasties. The Assyrian Empire, the Persian Empire, the empire of Alexander, were not homelands either. There were never Assyrian patriots; the Persian Empire was a vast feudality. No nation traces its origins to Alexander's colossal adventure, even though this was so rich in consequences for the general history of civilization.

The Roman Empire was far closer to being a homeland. In return for the immense benefit of ending wars, Roman domination, initially so harsh, came quickly to be loved. The empire was a great association of peace and civilization, synonymous with order. In the later periods of the empire there was among cultivated minds, enlightened bishops, the lettered classes, a genuine sentiment of *Pax Romana*, holding at bay the threatening chaos of barbarism. But an empire twelve times larger than present-day France could not form a state in the modern sense of the term. The division between East and West was unavoidable. The attempts at a Gallic empire in the third century of our era were unsuccessful. It was the Germanic invasions that introduced into the world the principle that would later serve as the basis for the existence of nationalities.

What did the Germanic peoples achieve, in fact, from their great invasions of the fifth century down to the last Norman conquests of the tenth century? They did not much change the racial stock; but they imposed dynasties and a military aristocracy on more or less considerable parts of the old empire of the West, which took the names of their invaders. So we had a France, a Burgundy, a Lombardy – later a Normandy. The rapid predominance that the Frankish empire acquired briefly remade the unity of the West; but that empire broke up irremediably around the middle of the ninth century; the Partition of Verdun traced a dividing line that was fundamentally immutable, and from this time on, France, Germany, England, Italy and Spain set out on the path, often circuitous and marked by countless adventures, towards their full national existence as we see this in full bloom today.

What then actually is the defining characteristic of these different states? It is the fusion of the populations that compose them. In the countries that we have just listed there is nothing analogous to what you will find in Turkey, where Turks, Slavs, Greeks, Armenians, Syrians and Kurds are as distinct today as at the time they were conquered. Two fundamental circumstances contributed to this result. First of all, the fact that the Germanic peoples adopted Christianity as soon as they had regular contact with the Greek and Latin peoples. When conqueror and conquered share the same religion, or rather, when the conqueror adopts the religion of the conquered, the Turkish system, in which an absolute distinction is made between men on the grounds of religion, can no longer arise. The second circumstance was the conquerors' forgetting of their own language. The grandsons of Clovis, Alaric, Gundebald,

Alboin and Rollo already spoke a Romanic tongue.[3] This fact was itself the consequence of a further very particular feature; the Franks, Burgundians, Goths, Lombards and Normans were accompanied by very few women of their race. For several generations, though their chiefs only married Germanic women, their concubines and their children's nurses were Latin – which meant that the *lingua francica* or the *lingua gothica* had but a short lease of life once the Franks and Goths were settled in Roman lands. The situation in England was different, as the Anglo-Saxon invaders certainly had women with them; the Celtic population fled, and moreover, Latin was no longer so dominant in Britain, or even had never been so. If Gallic had been generally spoken in Gaul in the fifth century, Clovis and his people would not have abandoned Germanic for this.

Hence the decisive result that, despite the extreme violence of the customs of the Germanic invaders, the mould that they imposed became over the centuries the actual mould of the nation. *France* became quite legitimately the name of a country in which only an imperceptible number of Franks had settled. By the tenth century, in the earliest *chansons de geste* that are such a perfect mirror

---

3   Alaric was king of the Visigoths from 395 to 410; Gundebald the Burgundian king from 480 to 516; Alboin was a Lombard king in the mid sixth century; Rollo (d. between 927 and 933) was the Viking chief who found the duchy of Normandy.

of their time, all the inhabitants of France are known as French. The idea of a difference of races in the French population, still so evident for Gregory of Tours,[4] is no longer present to any extent in French writers and poets later than the time of Hugues Capet. The difference between noble and serf is as marked as can possibly be, but this difference is in no way an ethnic one; it is a difference in courage, customs and education that is transmitted by inheritance, and the idea that the origin of all this lay in conquest did not occur to anyone. The spurious system according to which the nobility owed their origin to a privilege conferred by the king for great services to the nation, so that each noble had been ennobled, was established as a dogma in the thirteenth century. The same happened in the wake of almost all the Norman conquests. At the end of one or two generations, the Norman invaders were no longer distinct from the rest of the population, though their influence was no less profound. They had given the conquered country a nobility, military customs and a patriotism, which it had not previously possessed.

Forgetting, and I might even say historical error, is an essential factor in the creation of a nation, and this is why the progress of historical studies is often a danger to the principle of nationality. Historical investigation, in

---

4   Gregory, bishop of Tours, was historian of the church and the Franks (c. 538–94).

fact, brings to light the deeds of violence that took place at the origin of all political formations, even those whose consequences have been most fortunate. Unity is always achieved brutally; the union of northern France and the Midi was the result of an extermination and terror lasting for almost a century. The king of France who was, if I dare to say so, the ideal type of his kind [i.e. Philippe Augustus, 1165–1223]; the king of France who established the most complete national unity that there is; this king of France lost his prestige once he was examined too closely. The nation that he formed has cursed him, and today it is only educated minds who appreciate his merit and what he accomplished.

These great laws of the history of Western Europe become perceptible by way of contrast. The same undertaking that the king of France so admirably completed, partly by his tyranny, partly by his justice, many other countries failed to achieve. Under the crown of St Stephen,[5] Magyars and Slavs remain as distinct as they were eight centuries ago. Far from fusing together the diverse elements of its domains, the house of Habsburg kept them distinct and often opposed to one another. In Bohemia, the Czech element and the German are superimposed like oil and water in a glass. The Turkish policy of separating

5   Szent István was the founder of the Hungarian kingdom (c. 975–1038).

nationalities according to religion has had still more serious consequences, bringing about the ruin of the East. If
you take a city such as Smyrna or Salonica, you will find
five or six communities, each of which has its own memories and which have scarcely anything in common. The
essence of a nation, however, is that all individuals have
many things in common, including that they have equally
forgotten many things. No French citizen knows whether
he is Burgundian, Alan, Taifal or Visigoth; every French
citizen has to have forgotten St Bartholomew's night, or
the thirteenth-century massacres in the Midi.[6] There are
not ten families in France who can supply evidence of a
Frankish origin, and any such evidence would still be
essentially defective, after countless unknown conjuga-
tions capable of undermining any genealogical system.

The modern nation is thus a historical product brought
about by a series of convergent facts. Sometimes its
unity has been achieved by a dynasty, as was the case
with France; sometimes it has been by the direct will of a
number of provinces, as was the case with the Netherlands,
Switzerland and Belgium; sometimes by a general spirit
that belatedly overcame the caprices of feudalism, as is the
case with Italy and Germany. All such processes of formation have had a deep underlying rationality. These princi-
ples, in such cases, only come to light by way of the most

---

6   Renan alludes here to the massacres of the Cathars or Albigensians.

unexpected surprises. We have seen in our own time how Italy was unified by its defeats, and Turkey demolished by its victories. Every defeat brought progress in Italy, every victory was a further loss to Turkey; because Italy is a nation, and Turkey outside of Asia Minor is not one. It is the glory of France to have proclaimed, through the French Revolution, that a nation exists by way of itself. We cannot see it as a bad thing if others imitate us. The national principle is thus our own principle. But what then is a nation? Why is the Netherlands a nation, whereas Hanover or the Grand Duchy of Parma are not? How has France persisted in being a nation, when the principle that created it has disappeared? How is Switzerland a nation, with three languages, two religions, and three or four races, whereas Tuscany, for example, which is so homogeneous, is not? Why is Austria a state and not a nation? How does the principle of nationalities differ from the principle of races? These are points that a reflective mind needs to have settled, for the sake of consistency. The affairs of the world are hardly governed by such kinds of reasoning: but diligent men seek to bring some reason into these matters, and clarify the confusions that ensnare superficial minds.

II

To listen to certain political theorists, a nation is above all a dynasty, representing an ancient conquest – one first accepted by the mass of people and then forgotten. According to these theorists, the grouping of provinces effected by a dynasty, by its wars, marriages and treaties, ends along with the dynasty that formed it. It is quite true that the majority of modern nations were each created by a family of feudal origin, which contracted an alliance with the soil and which was in a way a kernel of centralization. The frontiers of France in 1789 had nothing natural or necessary about them. The wide zone that the house of Capet added to the narrow strip of the treaty of Verdun was indeed the personal acquisition of this house. At the time when these annexations were made, there was no idea either of natural frontiers, of the right of nations, or of the will of provinces. The union of England, Ireland and Scotland was likewise a dynastic deed. Italy took so long in becoming a nation only because, among its several ruling houses, none before our own century made itself the centre of unity. It is a strange fact that it took a royal title from the obscure island of Sardinia, a land scarcely even Italian. The Netherlands, which created itself by an act of heroic resolve, nevertheless contracted an intimate alliance with the house of Orange,[7] and it would run grave dangers the day that this union was compromised.

---

7   The house of Orange-Nassau has reigned over the Netherlands since the sixteenth century.

But is such a law at all absolute? Undoubtedly not. Switzerland and the United States, which were formed as conglomerates by successive additions, lack any dynastic base. I shall not discuss the question as far as France is concerned. One would have to be able to read the future. Let us simply say that the great French kingdom had been so highly national that, the day after its fall, the nation was able to persist without it. And then the eighteenth century changed everything. After centuries of abasement, man returned to the spirit of antiquity, to self-respect, to the idea of his rights. The words 'homeland' and 'citizen' regained their meaning. In this way the boldest operation practised in history could succeed, an operation that may be compared with what in physiology would be the attempt to revive in its original identity a body whose brain and heart had already been removed.

We have to admit, then, that a nation can exist without a dynastic principle, and even that nations that were formed by dynasties can separate from these dynasties without then ceasing to exist. The old principle that only takes account of the right of princes can no longer be maintained; besides dynastic right, there is national right. On what criterion can this national right be founded? By what sign should we recognize it? From what tangible fact can it be derived?

From race, many would say with assurance
For these people, artificial divisions resulting from feudalism, princely marriages and diplomatic congresses have

had their day. What remains fixed and firm is the race of a population. It is this that establishes right and legitimacy. The Germanic family, for example, according to the present theory, has the right to retake the scattered members of the Germanic lands, even when these members do not ask to rejoin it. The right of Germany over this or that province is stronger than the right of the province's own inhabitants over themselves. In this way a kind of primordial right is created, analogous to the divine right of kings; the principle of ethnography is substituted for that of nations. This is a very great mistake, which, if it came to prevail, would mean the end of European civilization. While the national principle is just and legitimate, the primordial right of races is narrow and full of danger for genuine progress.

In the tribe and the antique city the fact of race was of first importance, as we recognize. The tribe and the city were then no more than an extension of the family. In Sparta or Athens, all citizens were related to a greater or lesser degree. It was the same with the sons of Israel, and still is the case with the Arab tribes. Let us now turn from Athens and Sparta, from the Israelite tribe, to the Roman Empire. The situation there was quite different. Initially formed by violence, but then maintained by self-interest, this great agglomeration of cities and provinces, completely different from one another, struck the idea of race a most serious blow. Christianity, with its universal and absolute character, worked still more effectively in the same direction. It contracted an intimate alliance with the Roman Empire and, by the working of these two incomparable agents of unification, ethnographic argument was removed from the government of human affairs for many centuries.

The barbarian invasions, despite appearances, were a further step along this path. The demarcations of the barbarian kingdoms were in no way ethnographic, but governed by the strength and caprice of the invaders. The race of the populations they subjugated was for them a matter of complete indifference. Charlemagne remade in his own way what Rome had made already: a single empire composed of the most diverse races; and the authors of the treaty of Verdun, in calmly tracing two great lines from north to south, were not in the least concerned with the race of the peoples who found themselves on one side or the other. The changes in borders that took place in the course of the Middle Ages were likewise independent of any ethnographic development. If the policy followed by the house of Capet succeeded in gradually gathering, under the name of Franche, the territories of ancient Gaul, this was not an effect of a tendency on the part of these lands to rejoin their fellow nationals. The Dauphiné, Bresse, Provence and France-Comté no longer remembered a common origin. Any Gallic consciousness had disappeared by the second century of our era, and it is only by way of scholarship that the individuality of the Gallic character has been retrospectively rediscovered in our own day.

Ethnographic considerations thus counted for nothing in the constitution of modern nations. France is Celtic, Iberian and Germanic. Germany is Germanic, Celtic and Slav. Italy is the country where ethnography is most confused. Gauls, Etruscans, Pelasgians, Greeks, and many other elements besides, are crossed here in an indecipherable mixture. The British Isles, taken as a whole, offer a mixture of Celtic and Germanic blood, in proportions that are singularly difficult to determine.

The truth is that there is no pure race, and that to base politics on ethnographic analysis is to surrender it to a chimera. The noblest countries, England, France and Italy, are those where blood is most mixed. Is Germany an exception to this rule? Is it a purely Germanic country? What an illusion! The whole of the south was Gallic. The whole of the east, across the Elbe, is Slav. And as for the parts that are claimed to be genuinely pure, are they actually so? Here we come to one of the problems where it is most important to get ideas straight and avoid misunderstandings.

Discussions about races are interminable, because the word 'race' is used by philological historians and physiological anthropologists in two completely different senses.[8]

---

8   I have developed this point further in a lecture that was summarized in the bulletin of the Association Scientifique de France, 10 March 1878 [Renan's note].

For anthropologists, race has the same meaning as it does in zoology; it indicates an actual descent, an affinity of blood. But the study of languages and history does not lead to the same demarcations as does physiology. The words 'brachycephalic' and 'dolichocephalic' have no place either in history or philology.[9] In the human group that created the Aryan languages and way of life, there were already both brachycephalics and dolichocephalics. The same must be said of the original group that created those languages and institutions known as Semitic. In other words, the zoological origins of humanity are incomparably earlier than the origins of culture, civilization and language. The original Aryan, Semitic and Turanian groups lacked any physiological unity.[10] These groupings are historic facts that took place at a certain epoch, some fifteen or twenty thousand years ago, whereas the zoological origin of humanity is lost in incalculable shadows. What in philological or historical terms is called the Germanic race, is certainly a quite distinct family in the human species. But is it a family in the anthropological sense? Certainly not. The appearance of Germanic individuality in history occurred only a few centuries before Jesus Christ. At that time, it would seem, the Germanic peoples had not come into the world. Previously, mingled with the

---

9   'Brachycephalic' literally means short-headed, and 'dolichocephalic' long-headed. These terms were used by racist theories seeking to establish a hierarchical classification of 'human races'.

10   Turanian denotes the various Turkic peoples.

Slavs in the great indistinct mass of Scythians, they did not have their own individuality. An Englishman is certainly a particular type in humanity as a whole. But this type of what is quite improperly called the Anglo-Saxon race[11] is not the Briton of Caesar's time, nor the Anglo-Saxon of Hengist, nor the Dane of Knut, nor the Norman of William the Conqueror; it is rather the result of all these. The Frenchman is neither a Gaul, nor a Frank, nor a Burgundian. He is rather what emerged from the great vessel in which the most varied elements fermented together, presided over by the king of France. The inhabitants of Jersey or Guernsey differ in no way, in terms of their origins, from the Norman population of the adjacent coast. In the eleventh century, the most penetrating eye could not have noted the slightest difference between the two sides of the Channel. Only insignificant circumstances ensured that Philippe Augustus did not take these islands along with the rest of Normandy. After nearly seven centuries of separation, however, the two populations have become not only foreign to one another, but quite unmistakable. Race as we historians understand it is thus something that is made and unmade. The study of race is crucial for the scholar concerned with the history of

---

11   Germanic elements are not much greater in the United Kingdom than they were in France, at the time when it possessed Alsace and Metz. The Germanic tongue prevailed in the British Isles simply and solely because Latin had not completely replaced Celtic idioms, as it did among the Gauls [Renan's note].

humanity. It has no application in politics. The instinctive awareness that presided over the construction of the map of Europe took no account of race, and the leading European nations are essentially nations of mixed blood.

The fact of race, originally crucial, thus steadily loses its importance. Human history differs fundamentally from zoology. Race here is not everything, as with rodents or felines, and no one has the right to go round the world, fingering people's skulls and then seizing them by the throat and telling them: 'You have our blood, you belong to us!' Apart from anthropological characters, there is reason, justice, truth and beauty, which are the same for all. This ethnographic policy has no firm basis; if you use it today against others, you will see it turn against yourselves tomorrow. Is it certain that the Germans, who have raised so high the banner of ethnography, will not see the Slavs coming along and analysing, in their turn, the names of villages in Saxony or Lusatia, seeking traces of the Wiltzes or Obotrites,[12] and demanding compensation for the massacres and enslavement that the Ottos committed against their ancestors? It is good for everyone to be able to forget.

I am very fond of ethnography. It is a science of rare interest, but I want it to be independent, and free of any political application. In ethnography, as in all other studies, systems change; that is the condition of progress.

---

12   Slavic tribes settled in eastern Germany in the early Middle Ages.

The frontiers of states would then follow fluctuations in science. Patriotism would depend on a more or less paradoxical dissertation. One would have to say to the patriot: 'You were mistaken; you spilled your blood for that cause; you thought you were a Celt; no, you're a German.' Then, ten years later, you'll be told that you're a Slav. So as not to falsify science, let us dispense it from giving an opinion on questions where such great interest is engaged. You can be sure that, if it is charged with furnishing elements for diplomacy, it will often be surprised *in flagrante delicto*. It has better things to do; let us simply ask it for the truth.

What we have just said of race must also be said of language Language invites unification; it does not force this. The United States and England, Hispanic America and Spain, each speak a common language yet do not form a single nation. Switzerland, on the other hand, since it was composed by the consent of its different parts, counts three or four languages. There is in man something superior to language; that is will. The will of Switzerland to be united, despite the variety of its dialects, is a far more important fact than a similarity often obtained only by a lot of trouble.

One fact to the honour of France is that it has never sought to obtain unity of language by measures of coercion.[13] Is it not possible to have the same sentiments and

---

13   An astonishing claim, given that Renan was born in Brittany in 1823.

thoughts, to love the same things, in different languages?
We were just now saying how inconvenient it would be
to make international politics depend on ethnography. It
would be equally so to make it depend on comparative
philology. Let us leave these interesting studies complete
freedom in their discussions; let us not confuse these with
matters that disturb their serenity. The political importance ascribed to languages comes from the fact that they
are regarded as signs of race. Nothing could be more
wrong. Prussia, where only German is spoken now, spoke
a Slavic tongue a few centuries ago; Wales speaks English;
Gaul and Spain speak the original tongue of Alba Longa;[14]
Egypt speaks Arabic – examples are countless. Even originally, identity of language did not mean identity of race.
Let us take the proto-Aryan or proto-Semitic tribe; there
were slaves, who spoke the same language as their masters,
though the slave was very often from a different race than
his master. To repeat: the divisions of the Indo-European,
Semitic and other languages, established by comparative
philology with such admirable sagacity, do not coincide
with the divisions of anthropology. Languages are historical formations, which have very little to say about the
blood of those who speak them, and which, in any case,
could not shackle human freedom when it was a matter

---

14   The ancient fortified city of Latium, twenty kilometres south-east
of Rome.

of determining the family that one unites with for life and death.

An exclusive focus on language, like too strong an attention paid to race, also has its dangers and inconveniences. This exaggeration leads to isolation with a particular culture taken as national; people hem themselves in and shut the door. They leave the open air that is breathed in the wide field of humanity, to enclose themselves in conventicles of compatriots. Nothing is worse for the mind, or more vexing for civilization. Let us not abandon the fundamental principle that man is a rational and moral being prior to being a speaker of this or that language, a member of this or that culture. Before French culture, German culture or Italian culture, there is human culture. Look at the great men of the Renaissance; they were neither French, nor Italian, nor German. They had rediscovered, by their study of antiquity, the secret of the genuine education of the human mind, and devoted themselves to this body and soul. And how well they succeeded!

Nor can religion provide a sufficient basis for the establishment of a modern nationality
Originally, religion was a matter of the very existence of the social group, which was an extension of the family. Religion and rituals were family rites. The religion of Athens was the cult of Athens itself, of its mythical founders, its laws and customs. It did not imply any dogmatic theology. This

religion was, in the full sense of the term, a state religion. You were not an Athenian if you refused to practise it. It was at bottom the cult of the Acropolis personified. To swear on the altar of Aglauros[15] was to swear readiness to die for the *patrie*. This religion was the equivalent of what drawing lots [for military service] or the cult of the flag is for us. Refusing to participate in such a cult was what refusing military service would be in our day. It meant declaring that one was not Athenian. On the other hand, it is clear that this kind of cult meant nothing for someone who was not from Athens; so there was no proselytism to force foreigners to accept it, nor did the Athenian slaves practise it. The situation was the same in some of the small republics of the Middle Ages. You were not a good Venetian if you did not swear by St Mark; you were not a good Amalfitan if you did not place St Andrew above all the other saints in heaven. In these little societies, what was later seen as persecution and tyranny was quite legitimate, of no greater moment than our custom of sending your father birthday greetings or wishing him a Happy New Year.

What was the case in Sparta and Athens was no longer so in the kingdoms that emerged from Alexander's conquests, and still less so under the Roman Empire. The persecutions by which Antiochus Epiphanes sought

---

15   Aglauros was the Acropolis itself, devoted to saving the fatherland [Renan's note].

to win the East to the cult of Olympian Jupiter, or those of the Roman Empire designed to maintain a proclaimed state religion, were a mistake, a crime, a genuine absurdity. In our own day, the situation is perfectly clear. There are no longer masses of people who believe in a uniform way. Each person believes and practises as they see fit, whatever they want or like. There is no longer a state religion; you can be French, English or German while being Catholic, Protestant, Jewish or not practising any religion. Religion has become something individual, a matter for each person's conscience. There is no longer the division between Catholic and Protestant nations. Religion, which only fifty-two years ago was such a major element in the formation of Belgium, keeps its full importance in each person's inner life; but it has almost completely disappeared from the causes that draw divisions between peoples.

Community of interest is certainly a powerful tie between people
Is self-interest, however, sufficient to make for a nation? I do not believe this. Community of interest only makes commercial treaties. There is an aspect of sentiment in nationality; it is body and soul together; a *Zollverein* is not a fatherland.[16]

---

16   The *Zollverein* was the customs and free-trade union formed in 1833–4 by the majority of states in the German Confederation.

Geography, and what are called natural frontiers, certainly
plays a considerable part in the division of nations

Geography is one of the fundamental factors of history.
Rivers have led races on; mountains have halted them. The
former favoured historic movements, the latter limited
them. But is it possible to say, as certain parties believe,
that the limits of a nation are written on the map, and that
one nation has the right to judge what is necessary for it, to
round off awkward corners or incorporate a certain mountain or river that is ascribed a kind of limiting faculty *a
priori*? I know of no doctrine so arbitrary or harmful. It
makes it possible to justify any kind of violence. And to
start with, do such mountains or rivers really form these
supposed natural borders? It is incontestable that mountains separate; but rivers rather unite. And then not all
mountains have been able to divide states. Which ones
separate and which do not? Between Biarritz and Tornea
there is not one estuary that has more than any other the
character of a frontier. If history had wanted, then the
Loire, the Seine, the Meuse, the Elbe or the Oder might
have had, along with the Rhine, the same character of a
natural frontier that has led to so many infractions of the
basic law that is the will of men. People talk of strategic
reasons. Nothing is absolute; it is clear that many concessions must be made to necessity. But these concessions
must not go too far. Otherwise the whole world will claim
its military requirements, and there will be war without

end. No, it is not land any more than race that makes a nation. Land provides the substratum, the field of struggle and work; man provides the soul. Man is everything in the formation of that sacred thing called a people. Nothing material can suffice. A nation is a spiritual principle resulting from profound complications of history, a spiritual family and not a group determined by the configuration of the soil.

We have seen, then, what does not suffice to create such a spiritual principle: race, language, interests, religious affinity, geography, military necessity. What then is needed? Following from what I have said before, I shall not need to keep your attention much longer.

III

A nation is a soul, a spiritual principle. Two things that, in truth, are only one, make up this soul, this spiritual principle. One of these lies in the past, the other in the present. One is the possession in common of a rich legacy of memories; the other is the present consent, the desire to live together, the will to continue to validate the heritage that has been jointly received. Man is not improvised, gentlemen. The nation, like the individual, is the culmination of a long past of effort, sacrifice and devotion. This makes the cult of ancestors all the more legitimate; it is our ancestors who made us what we are. A heroic past, great men, glory (genuine glory, I mean), that is the social capital on which a national idea is founded. To have common glories in the past, and a common will in the present; to have done great things together, and to seek to do so again, those are the essential conditions for being a people. One loves in proportion to the sacrifices to which one has consented, the evils that one has suffered. One loves the house that one has built and passes on. The Spartan song 'We are what you were; we shall be what you are' is, in its simplicity, the summary hymn of every homeland.

In the past, a heritage of shared glory and regrets, in the future a similar programme to be realized; to have suffered, enjoyed and hoped together – that is worth more than customs unions and frontiers that match strategic ideas; this is what is understood despite differences of race and language. I said just now: 'to have suffered together'; yes, common suffering unites more than does joy. National memories, in fact, and national griefs, are worth more than triumphs, as they impose duties and command common effort.

A nation is thus a great solidarity, constituted by the sentiment of the sacrifices that have been made and by those that people are ready to make again. It presupposes a past, yet it is summed up in the present by a tangible fact: the clearly expressed consent and desire to continue a common life. The existence of a nation is, if you will pardon me the metaphor, a daily plebiscite, just as the existence of an individual is a perpetual affirmation of life. I do indeed realize that this is less metaphysical than divine right, less brutal than a supposed historical right. In the order of ideas that I propose to you, a nation does not have any more right than a king to say to a province: 'You belong to me, I am taking you.' A province, for us, means its inhabitants; if anyone has the right to be consulted in this matter, it is the inhabitants. A nation never has a genuine interest in annexing or retaining a country against its will. The will of nations is definitively the sole legitimate criterion, to which one must always return.

We have expelled metaphysical and theological abstractions from politics. What remains after this? There remains man, his desires and his needs. The secession of nations, you may tell me, and in the long run their fragmentation, is the result of a system that puts these old organisms at the mercy of wills that are often little enlightened. It is clear that in a matter of this kind, no principle should be pushed to excess. Truths of this order are only applicable as a whole, and in a very general manner. Human wills change – but what does not change on this earth? Nations are not something eternal. They had a beginning and will have an end. It is probable that a European confederation will replace them. But this is not the law of the century in which we are living. At the present time, the existence of nations is good and even necessary. Their existence is the guarantee of freedom, which would be lost if the world had only one law and one master.

Through their various and often opposing faculties, nations serve the common work of civilization: they all sound their own note in the great concert of humanity which is, in the last analysis, the highest ideal reality that we can reach. Each by itself has its weak points. I often tell myself that an individual with the faults that are taken in nations as qualities, an individual fuelled by such vainglory, and so jealous, egoistic and quarrelsome, an individual always ready to draw the sword rather than tolerate, would be the most insufferable of men. But all these discordant details disappear in the whole. Poor humanity, what you have suffered! What tests still await you! May the spirit of wisdom guide you and preserve you from the countless dangers that beset your road!

To sum up, gentlemen. Man is neither the slave of his race nor his language, neither of his religion nor of the course of rivers, nor yet of the direction of mountain ranges. A great aggregation of men, healthy in mind and warm in heart, creates that moral consciousness that we call a nation. As long as this moral consciousness proves its strength by the sacrifices that are required by the abdication of the individual to the benefit of a community, it is legitimate and has the right to exist. If doubts arise as to its frontiers, consult the populations in dispute. They certainly have the right to an opinion on the matter. This will certainly raise a smile on the part of the geniuses of politics, those infallible beings who pass their lives deceiving themselves, and take pity on our mundane existence from the height of their superior principle. 'Consult the populations indeed! What naivety! A pathetic French idea that wants to replace diplomacy and war by methods of childish simplicity!' – Be wary, gentlemen; let us leave behind the reign of such geniuses; let us be able to accept the disdain of the strong. Perhaps, after so much fruitless experimentation, people will come back to our modest empirical solutions. The way to be right in the future is sometimes to be able to resign oneself to being out-of-date.

Judaism as Race and Religion

Ernest Renan

Lecture given to the Cercle Saint-Simon, 27 January 1883

Gentlemen,

Your generous reception touches me more than I can say; but the solemn character of this platform troubles me somewhat. I had agreed to speak to you this evening on condition that our discussion would be just a simple exchange of views, without oratorical artifice. I find the stenographic apparatus intimidating, as what I wanted was simply to think aloud, as it were, in your presence on one of the subjects that has most often attracted my study in recent years. I claim your indulgence for a presentation that was not designed, as I saw it, to be more than a simple conversation, and that your kind insistence has transformed into a lecture. The subject speaks for itself, and will bear me out.

I would like to exchange a few ideas with you on the distinction that I believe it is important to make between the religious question and the ethnographic question, as far as Judaism is concerned. It is as clear as day that Judaism is a religion, and a great one. But people generally go further. They consider Judaism a fact of race, and talk of the 'Jewish race'; they assume, in a word, that the Jewish people, who originally created this religion, have always kept it for themselves. They can certainly see that Christianity broke away from it at a certain time; but they continue happily to believe that this tiny creative people remained always identical, so that a Jew by religion must always be a Jew by blood. How far is this true? To what extent is it necessary to modify this conception? We shall examine this matter. But first of all, permit me to make the question as clear as possible by way of a comparison.

There exists in the world, in Bombay, the small religious group of the Parsees, the ancient religion of Persia. In this case, the question is perfectly clear. Parseeism is a religion that was national in origin, and is today maintained by a race that is almost homogeneous; I do not believe there have ever been, in fact, many conversions to Parseeism. Here, then, a religious fact is precisely congruent with a fact of race.

Let us then take, on the contrary, Protestantism in the countries where it is in a minority, such as France. Here the situation is the very opposite; there is no ethnographic fact. Why is a man Protestant? Because his ancestors were. And why were his ancestors? Because in the sixteenth century they happened to have an intellectual and moral disposition that led them to adopt the reformed church. Ethnography has nothing to say about such a case, and it would be vain to say that those who became Protestants in the sixteenth century did so for some racial reason. That would be a subtlety, or at least a consideration, of a different order than those with which we are concerned here.

In Parseeism, on the other hand, there certainly is an ethnographic fact; since, I repeat, there is very little spirit of proselytism in this small religious association located in Bombay.

What then is the situation with Judaism? Is it something analogous to Protestantism, or rather an ethnographic religion like Parseeism? This is the point on which I would like to reflect with you today.

There is a basic principle that will not detain me too long, gentlemen. I am speaking before people who are familiar with science, and the principle in question is more or less the ABC of the science of religions: it is the distinction between national or local religions, and universal ones.

There are in fact only three universal religions. There is first of all Buddhism, or one might better say Hinduism, since it is now very clear how before the propagation of Buddhism there was a propagation of Hinduism. The ancient monuments of Indo-China are not Buddhist, they are Brahman, and Buddhism only arrived there later; but it is above all in the Buddhist form, we acknowledge, that the Hindu religion made its conquests. The second universal religion is Christianity, and the third Islam. These are three great facts that have nothing ethnographic about them; there are Buddhists, Christians and Muslims of all races. We know at least approximately the dates at which these three religions appeared in the world. Buddhism goes back four or five centuries before Jesus Christ; its great conquests came later. As for Christianity and Islam, the time of their respective formation is not in any doubt.

Apart from these universal religions, however, there have been thousands of local and national ones. Athens had its religion, Sparta had its religion, all the nations of antiquity had their religions. Places, in the ancient world, equally had their religions. That was one of the most deep-rooted ideas of antiquity. In the second and third centuries of our era, the constant argument of Celsius[17] and the opponents of Christianity was that countries have gods that protect them and are concerned for their destiny.

This old idea is expressed in the most naïve fashion in a story in the second book of Kings, regarding the situation of the men of Cuth, who had been brought to Samaria by the Assyrians. Among the misfortunes that beset them, they

---

17   Celsius was an Epicurean philosopher of the second century CE.

were attacked by lions, which they saw as emissaries from the god of the country who was displeased at not being worshipped in the proper fashion. They sent the Assyrian government a petition, which is more or less summed up as follows: 'The god of the country is vexed with us because he is not served as he would wish to be. Send us priests who know how we may satisfy him.'[18] This is certainly a very different idea from that of Christianity or Buddhism. The god here is essentially local and provincial.

All these local or national religions have perished. Humanity increasingly desired universal religions, that explained to man his general duties and claimed to teach humanity the secret of its destiny. National religions had a more limited programme: this was patriotism combined with the idea that each country has a spirit that watches over it and demands to be served in a certain manner. This narrow theology has completely disappeared. It disappeared in the face of the Christian, Buddhist and Islamic ideas. That was a tremendous advance. I can hardly see,

---

18 'The king was told that the deported peoples whom he had settled in the cities of Samaria did not know the established usage of the god of the country, and that he had sent lions among them which were preying upon them because they did not know this. The king of Assyria, therefore, gave orders that one of the priests deported from Samaria should be sent back to live there and teach the people the usage of the god of the country. So one of the deported priests came and lived at Bethel, and taught them how they should pay their homage to the LORD' (2 Kings 17: 26–8).

in the history of civilized nations, more than two examples of ancient national religions that have survived; first of all Parseeism (and it has to be said that Parseeism offers its devotees many universal features), and then Judaism, which in a certain conception was the religion of a country, the land of Israel or the land of Judah, preserved by the descendants of that country's inhabitants.

I repeat here that this fact must be examined very closely indeed. There is absolutely no doubt that Judaism, the Israelite religion, was in its origin a national religion. It was the religion of the sons of Israel, and for many centuries was not fundamentally different from that of the neighbouring peoples, for example the Moabites. Yahweh, the Israelite god, protected Israel, just as Chemosh, the Moabite god, protected Moab. We know very well what the religious sentiment of a Moabite was, since the discovery of the inscription by King Mesha that is now in the Louvre, and in which this ruler of the ninth century BCE expressed, as it were, his private religious thoughts.[19] I certainly believe that the ideas of David were very much the same as those of Mesha. There was an intimate connection between Mesha and his god, Chemosh: Chemosh intervened at every point in the life of the king, giving him orders and advice; Chemosh brought the king all his victories; the king made fine sacrifices to him and laid before

---

19   The stele of Mesha, a stone of black basalt, was discovered in 1868.

him the sacred vessels of vanquished gods. He rewarded the god in proportion to what the god had given him; this was a religion of tit for tat. The religion of Israel, likewise, undoubtedly remained for a long time an egoistic and self-interested religion, the religion of a particular god, Yahweh.

What then made this cult of Yahweh into the universal religion of the civilized world? It was the prophets, around the eighth century BCE. That is the true glory of Israel. We have no evidence that there were also prophets among Israel's more or less closely related neighbours, the Phoenicians for example. There were certainly *nabis*, who were consulted when a donkey went missing or when you wanted to discover a secret. These were sorcerers. But Israel's *nabis* were something quite other. They were the founders of pure religion. Around the eighth century BCE we see the appearance of these men, the most illustrious of whom was Isaiah, who were not at all priests, and whose message was: 'Sacrifices are useless; God takes no pleasure in them. How can you have such a low idea of the deity that you do not understand that he finds these smells of burning fat repulsive? Be just, and worship God with clean hands; that is the service he demands of you.' I do not believe that, in the time of King Mesha or King David, this line of thought was at all common. In those days, religion was simply an exchange of services and homage between the god and his servant; the eighth-century prophets, on the other hand, proclaimed that the true servant of Yahweh was the man who did good. Religion became in this way something moral and universal; it was permeated by the idea of justice, and it is for this that the prophets of Israel are the most scathing tribunes there have ever been, all the more so in that they had no conception of a future life to console themselves, and it was here below, in their view, that justice must reign.

Here we have the appearance of something unique in the world, pure religion. You see, in fact, how a religion of this kind has nothing national about it. When you worship a god who made heaven and earth, who loves good and punishes evil (the latter being rather hard to prove without the idea of a life beyond the grave, but they did their best to do so); when you proclaim such a religion you are no longer in the confines of nationality, you are in full human consciousness, in the widest sense. These great founders went on to draw the full consequences of their doctrine, consequences that would have ended in suppressing sacrifices and the Temple. They would have reached this point . . . What am I saying? They did reach this point, as the founders of Christianity were the last representatives of the prophetic spirit, and Christianity proclaims that sacrifices are something absolutely archaic that should no longer exist in religion according to the spirit.

As for the Temple, the founder of Christianity was accused of having spoken against it; did he really do so?

We shall never know. But in any case, an event occurred that settled the question: the destruction of the Temple by the Romans. This destruction was an immense benefit, as it is doubtful whether Christianity would have managed to detach itself completely from the Temple, if the Temple had remained.

I repeat, the first founder of Christianity was Isaiah, around 725 BCE. By introducing into the Israelite world the idea of a moral religion, the idea of justice and the secondary value of sacrifices, Isaiah preceded Jesus by seven hundred years. This idea of pure religion was combined, in the prophets of that time, with a concept of a kind of golden age already visible in the future. The characteristic feature of Israel is the persistent proclamation of a brilliant future for humanity, in which justice will reign on earth, in which inferior, crude and idolatrous cults will disappear. This can be found in the authentic sections of Isaiah. You are aware that the work of this prophet has to be delicately analysed. The latter part of the book attributed to him is posterior to the Babylonian captivity, but the chapters that I have in mind here, chapters 11, 19, 23 and 32, for example, are undoubtedly the work of Isaiah himself, and it is here that there is most insistence on the conversion of the pagans of Egypt, Tyre and Assyria.

Idolatry will therefore disappear from the world, it will do so by the action of the Jewish people; the Jewish people will then be a 'banner' that the nations will see on the horizon, and around which they will come and rally. The messianic or sibylline ideal was thus laid down in its essential lines well before the Babylonian captivity. Israel dreams a future of happiness for humanity, a perfect kingdom whose capital will be Jerusalem, where all nations will come to pay homage to the Lord. It is clear that a religion of this kind is not national. It cannot be denied that there is at the base of all this a share of national pride: what historical achievement is free from this? But the idea, as you can see, is universal first of all, and from here to propaganda and preaching is only a single step. The world at this time was not ready for large-scale propaganda like the later Christian apostolate. The missions of St Paul, the connections between the different churches, only became possible with the Roman Empire. But the notion of a universal religion was none the less born at the heart of ancient Israel. It was expressed far more energetically in the writings of the captivity. The century that followed the destruction of Jerusalem was an era of wonderful blossoming for the Jewish spirit. Remember the fine chapters that were appended to the book of Isaiah: 'Arise, Jerusalem, rise clothed in light; your light has come and the glory of the Lord shines over you.'[20] Remember again the image of Zechariah: 'In those days, when ten men from nations of every language pluck up courage, they shall pluck the robe

---

20   Isaiah 60: 1.

of a Jew and say, "Take us to Jerusalem; that is where true sacrifices are made, the only ones that the Lord accepts."'[21] The light thus emanates from the Jewish people, and this light will fill the whole world. An idea like this has nothing ethnographic about it: it is in the highest degree universal, and the people who proclaim it are clearly called to a destiny that goes beyond many of the bounds of a determined national role.

What then happened, in terms of race, during the captivity and especially during the long period of Persian domination, from about 530 BCE through to Alexander? We do not know. Was there much ethnic mixing in Israel at this time? It would be bold to assert this; but on the other hand, we cannot avoid recognizing this possibility. The barrier surrounding Israel must have undergone more than one breach during this time of disorganization. I can see only one single fact that might relate to the subject that concerns us here – the deep aversion that the reformers Nehemiah and Ezra had towards mixed marriages. This was a real *idée fixe* with them. It is likely that among the groups of Jews who returned from the east there were more men than women, forcing the immigrants to take wives from the neighbouring tribes. These unions were

---

21   Zechariah 8: 23. The wording of the last sentence here in New English Bible is: 'We will go with you because we have heard that God is with you.'

forbidden from the point of view of religion; but the strong prohibition itself makes it likely that they took place on a large scale.

A further significant fact is what is said about the kingdom of Samaria, which, we are told, was also peopled by foreigners following its destruction by the Assyrians. There is probably some exaggeration here. According to the accounts in the books of Kings, the country was deserted, which is scarcely likely. But it can hardly be doubted that colonists brought in by the Assyrians introduced into the Israelite population many elements that had nothing in common with them.

Let us come then to the Greek and Roman periods. This is the time when Jewish proselytism was in full swing; the time when the ethnography of the Jewish people, which had up to then been confined within quite narrow limits, suddenly expanded and admitted a crowd of foreign elements. My audience here is too well read for there to be any need for me to dwell on details. Everyone knows how active this Jewish propaganda was throughout the Greek era, both in Antioch and in Alexandria.

As far as Antioch is concerned, I would like to draw your attention to a passage from Flavius Josephus that has always struck me as very odd. In *The Wars of the Jews* (VII, 3, 3), Josephus speaks of the extraordinary prosperity of the Jews of Antioch, and says (I translate his words literally): 'Having brought to their cult a large number of Hellenes, they made them a part of their community.'[22]

What is involved here, therefore, is not just people living the Jewish life, as was the case later on in Rome, of uncircumcised proselytes; rather, a 'large number of Hellenes' (πολύ πλῆος) who converted to Judaism and became part of the synagogue. These were not half-Jews, like the philo-Judaic Flavians; they were people who became Jews and accepted the key act of initiation into Judaism, i.e. circumcision.

In Alexandria the situation was quite different. The Jewish church in Alexandria was certainly recruited largely from the Egypto-Hellenic community; Hebrew was soon forgotten. It was here that the enormous production of books took place that preceded Christianity; this was where those sibylline oracles saw the light, the false classical authors supposed to preach monotheism. The aim was to convert the pagans at all costs, and the propagandists, in their zeal, found no better way than to ascribe to ancient writers who were established authorities works in which the right doctrines were taught. This was also how the *Pseudo-Phocylides* and *Pseudo-Heraclitus* were fabricated, with the intention of preaching a diluted Judaism, reduced to a kind of natural religion.

---

22   http://www.gutenberg.org/files/2850/2850.txt has a variant.

The fact of this extraordinary propaganda of Judaism,
from around 150 BCE through to 200 CE, is incontestable. But, you will say, what proves too much proves too
little. The result of this proselytism, for Judaism, was far
more religious than ethnographic. People converted in
this way rarely had themselves circumcised. What was
called in Rome *vitam judaicam agere* simply means keeping
the Sabbath and practising Jewish morality. People who
'feared God', the *metuentes*, *ςεβομενοι*, *judoei improvessi*,
did not remain Jews; they simply passed through Judaism
on their way to Christianity.

Undoubtedly, by far the greater part of these Greeks
who adopted the Jewish life without circumcision
went on to become Christians. It was among them that
Christianity found its original ground. But it is equally
certain that a very large number of these people became
genuine Jews.

You have had evidence of this in the passage from
Josephus that I read you just now. I could also cite several
other facts, for example that of the women of Damascus
who, according to Josephus, were all Jewish at one
time.[23] Syria was the theatre of an immense propaganda
effort. My fellow scholar, M. Joseph Derenbourg,[24] has

---

23   'Almost all of them addicted to the Jewish religion' (II, 20, 2).
24   Franco-German historian and Orientalist (1881–95), Derenbourg
published in 1867 an *Essai sur l'histoire et la géographie de la Palestine
d'après les Talmuds et les autres sources rabbiniques*.

established this perfectly clearly. We have direct evidence from Palmyra, Iturea and Hauran. There is no story more familiar than that of Helena, queen of Adiabene,[25] who converted to Judaism along with her whole family; and it is very likely that a large part of the population followed the example of the dynasty. In all these cases, we have not just θεοσβεις, people who 'loved the Jews', but complete and circumcised Jews.

If the large scale of conversions to Judaism in the Greek and Latin countries is denied, it would still be impossible to deny this for the East, and Syria in particular. In Palmyra, for example, the inscriptions have a very pronounced Jewish character.

The Hasmonean and Herodian dynasties both contributed a great deal to this religious current, which brought to Judaism a mass of Syrian elements. The Hasmoneans were conquerors, who more or less reconstituted by force the old domain of Israel. There were non-Jews among the population there, including many pagans. They were conquered by John Hyrcanus, by Alexander Jannaeus, and forced to accept circumcision. The *'compelle intrare'* was quite violent in this case.[26] Under the Herodians, other means were used. The Herodians were an extremely rich family, and the bait of attractive marriages led many petty

---

25 See note on p. 26
26 'Make them come in', in the New English Bible (Luke 14: 23).

Eastern princes, those of Emessa, Cicilia and Commagene, to convert to Judaism. There were thus a considerable number of conversions, so much so that it is impossible to exaggerate the degree to which Syria was actually Judaized.

Allow me to read to you on this subject a passage from Josephus's treatise *Against Apion* (II, 39):

Nay, further, the multitude of mankind itself have had a great inclination of a long time to follow our religious observances; for there is not any city of the Grecians, nor any of the barbarians, nor any nation whatsoever, whither our custom of resting on the seventh day hath not come, and by which our fasts and lighting up lamps, and many of our prohibitions as to our food, are not observed; they also endeavour to imitate our mutual concord with one another, and the charitable distribution of our goods, and our diligence in our trades (*το φιλεργον εν ταις τέχναιςέ*), and our fortitude in undergoing the distresses we are in, on account of our laws; and, what is here matter of the greatest admiration, our law hath no bait of pleasure to allure men to it, but it prevails by its own force; and as God himself pervades all the world, so hath our law passed through all the world also. So that if any one will but reflect on his own country, and his own family, he will have reason to give credit to what I say.[27]

---

27   *The Works of Flavius Josephus*, trans. William Whiston, London 1987, p. 559.

We should note here this φιλεργον εν ταις τέχναιςέ, 'our diligence in our trades'. Jews and Christians, in fact, tended to be active in artisanal work. They were good workers. This was one of the secrets of the social revolution of Christianity, the rehabilitation of free labour.

There is a certain amount of exaggeration in this passage from Josephus; he was much given to this fault, but the general fact that he indicates certainly has its true side.

Here now is a passage from Dio Cassius, who was writing around 225 CE. He was a statesman, a senator, well acquainted with his time, and is speaking here of one of the Judean wars:

> [. . .] the country has been named Judaea, and the people themselves Jews. I do not know how this title came to be given them, but it applies also to all the rest of mankind, although of alien race (χαίπερ ἀλλοεθνεῖς ὄντες), who affect their customs. This class exists even among the Romans, and though often repressed has increased to a very great extent and has won its way to the right of freedom in its observances.[28]

This passage is clear: Dio Cassius knows that there are Jews by race, who continue their ancient tradition, but

---

28 *Dio's Roman History*, book 37, chapters 16–17 (London 1927, pp. 126–7).

that there are also Jews who are not so by blood, yet are none the less absolutely like Jews in terms of their religious observance.

In is unchallengeable that many people attracted to monotheism remained in the kind of deism whose perfect expression we find in the sibylline texts or in *Pseudo-Phocylides*,[29] an odd little book, a kind of moral treatise for pagans of which we have a Christian version in the prescriptions of what is known as the council of Jerusalem. This diluted Judaism, made for the use of Gentiles, abolished the great obstacle to conversion that was circumcision.

Thanks to Christian preaching, this had a tremendous success. But what must absolutely be borne in mind is that, on the other hand, a large number of converts had themselves circumcised and became Jews according to the conditions imposed on the supposed descendants of Abraham.

Let me read you now a passage from Juvenal (*Satires* XIV, 95 ff.), every word of which deserves to be weighed:

> Quidam sortiti metuentem sabbata patrem
> Nil praeter nubes et caeli numem adorant,
> Nec distare putant humana carne suillam,

29　Cf. Valentin Nikiprowetszky, *La Troisième Sibylle*, Paris 1970, as well as Walter T. Wilson, *The Sentences of Pseudo-Phocylides*, New York 2005.

Qua pater abstinuit, mox et praeputia ponunt;

Romanas autem soliti contemnere leges,

Judaïcum ediscunt et servant ac metuunt jus,

Tradidit arcano quodcumque volumine Moses:

Non monstrare vias eadem nisi sacra colenti,

Quaesitum ad fontem solos deducere verpos.

Sed pater in causa est cui septima quaeque fuit lux

Ignava et partem vitae non attigit ullam.[30]

So, it starts with a father who is a simple 'God-fearer' and confines himself to observing the Sabbath; but the son of this *metuens* becomes a Jew in the full sense of the term, and even a fanatical Jew with contempt for things Roman.

Juvenal's elaboration is probably slanderous. I do not believe that many Jews at this time were so fanatical as not to enlighten those who were not of their religion. But what does it signify? History is never spotless. The history of the Jewish people is one of the finest that there is, and I do not regret having devoted my life to it. But I am far from

---

30   'Some who have had a father who reveres the Sabbath, worship nothing but the clouds, and the divinity of the heavens, and see no difference between eating swine's flesh, from which their father abstained, and that of man; and in time they take to circumcision. Having been wont to flout the laws of Rome, they learn and practise and revere the Jewish law, and all that Moses committed to his secret tome, forbidding to point out the way to any not worshipping the same rite, and conducting none but the circumcised to the desired fountain. For all which the father was to blame, who gave up every seventh day to idleness, keeping it apart from all the concerns of life' (Trans. Ramsay).

claiming that it is absolutely without stain; that would not be a human history. If I could live a second life, I would certainly devote this to Greek history, which in certain respects is even finer than the Jewish. These are in a sense the two key histories of the world. And if I were to write a history of the Greek peoples, that history which is the most marvellous of all, I would not refuse to point out its unpleasant sides. One can admire Greece without being obliged to admire Creon and the dark pages in the annals of Athenian demagogy. In the same way, because one believes the Jewish people to have been perhaps the most extraordinary phenomenon in history, one is not obliged to deny that there have been some regrettable deeds in their long life as a people.

Let us not take Juvenal's accusations for more than they are worth; but let us none the less follow his reasoning. The evil, according to him, is that Roman society is being led towards Judaism. Why are there so many people who have abandoned the Roman tradition and adopted the Jewish one? The fault lies with those who started by embracing Jewish practices, without going as far as circumcision. The fathers observed the Sabbath, they were simple *metuentes*, men who feared God; the sons have themselves circumcised and become ardent Jews.

You see how the great propaganda work that was carried out from Alexander's time until around the third century of the Common Era was above all to the benefit of Christianity (this is beyond doubt), but also to the benefit of narrow Judaism, implying the rigorous practices of the old religion of Israel. It is true that the world, at a certain point, lost its taste for the old national religions and converted from paganism to monotheism. I have cited a number of texts on this, and I could cite more. '*Transgressi in morem eorum*', Tacitus says, '*idem usurpant*' (*History*, v, 5).[31] This refers to circumcision. According to Tacitus, those who go over to Judaism have themselves circumcised. There were therefore, among the converts, people who led the Jewish life without being circumcised, and others who were genuine Jews.

A deeply significant distinction is that established by a law of Antoninus the Pious, as commented on by Herrennius Modestinus.[32] Antoninus allowed Jews to circumcise their sons, but *only their sons*. I repeat, when authority is led to prohibit a practice, it is because that practice is widespread and has acquired a considerable scale.

I believe, gentlemen, that these facts sufficiently establish how, in the Greek and Roman eras, there was a plethora of direct conversions to Judaism. It follows from this that from this time on the word 'Judaism' scarcely still has

---

31 'Those who adopt their religion [the proselytes] follow the same practice.'
32 Herrennius was a jurisconsult of the third century CE.

any ethnographic meaning. Conforming to the predictions of the prophets, Judaism had become something universal. The whole world entered in. The movement that drew away from paganism, in the first centuries of our era, those persons inspired by delicate religious sentiments, brought a crowd of conversions. The greater part of these were certainly to Christianity, but a very large number also to Judaism. The majority of the Jews in Gaul and Italy, for example, must have come from such conversions, and the synagogue remained alongside the Christian church as a dissident minority.

It is true that the great Talmudic reaction occurred after this, in the wake of the war of Bar-Kokhba.[33] This is almost always how it happens in history: when a great and broad current of ideas is produced, those who were the first to provoke it become its first victims; they then almost repent of what they did, and, from being excessively liberal, become amazingly conservative. The Talmud represents such a reaction. Judaism felt it had gone too far, that it was going to collapse and dissolve into Christianity. And so it tightened its ranks. From this time on, proselytism disappears, and the proselytes are treated as a plague, the 'leprosy of Israel'. But before then, I repeat, the gates were wide open.

---

33   Simon Bar Koziba (or Bar-Kokhba) was the leader of the last Judean revolt against the Roman Empire, in 132–5 CE.

Did even Talmudism completely close these gates? Certainly not: proselytism, condemned by the doctors of the synagogue, still continued to be practised by pious laymen, more faithful to the ancient spirit than were the puritans of the Torah. It is simply that from now on we have to make a distinction. Orthodox Jews, rigorous observers of the Law, closed their ranks and, since the law could only be well observed in a tightly closed religious society, they systematically sequestered themselves from the rest of the world for centuries. Outside the scrupulous Talmudists, however, there were Jews with relatively broad ideas.

I know nothing more curious in this respect than the sermons of St John Chrysostomos[34] against the Jews. The background of the discussion in his sermons does not have great interest; but the orator, then a priest in Antioch, shows himself constantly obsessed by a fixed idea – to prevent the faithful from going to the synagogue to take an oath or celebrate the Pascal festival. It is clear that the division into two sects had still hardly taken place in the great city of Antioch.

Gregory of Tours has preserved for us invaluable information on Judaism among the Gauls. There were many Jews in Paris, Orléans and Clermont. Gregory fought

---

34   Archbishop of Constantinople, and one of the fathers of the Greek church in the late fourth century.

them as heretics. The idea did not occur to him that they were people of a different race. You will say that a simple mind like his was not familiar with ethnography. That is true; but where did these Paris or Orléans Jews come from? Can we imagine that they were all descendants of Orientals who came from Palestine at a certain time and established colonies of a kind in certain cities? I do not think so. No doubt there were Jewish immigrants in Gaul who had come up the Rhône and the Saône and acted in some sense as a leaven; but there were also a wealth of people who had attached themselves to Judaism by conversion and did not have a single ancestor in Palestine. When we recall that the Jewish communities of Germany and England came from France, we begin to regret not having more information on the origins of Judaism in our country. We would probably find that the Gallic Jew in the time of Gontran and Chilperic was most often simply a Gaul who practised the Jewish religion.

Let us leave aside these obscure facts; there are many that are perfectly clear. First of all, the conversion of Arabia and Abyssinia, which no one denies. In Arabia, Judaism made immense conquests before the time of Mohammed; a great many Arabs were attracted to it. It was touch and go that Arabia did not become Jewish. Mohammed had been a Jew at a certain period in his life, and we can say that up to a certain point he always remained one. The Falashas, or Abyssinian Jews, are Africans who speak an African language and read the Bible translated into an African tongue.[35]

There is however a more important historical event that is closer to us, and that seems to have had very major consequences: the conversion of the Khazars, on which we do have precise information. The Khazar kingdom, which occupied almost the whole of southern Russia, adopted Judaism around the time of Charlemagne. This historic act also brought in its wake the Karaites of southern Russia, and is seen in the Hebrew inscriptions of the Crimea, where from the eighth century there are Tartar and Turkish names such as Toktamish. Was a Jew of Palestinian origin ever called Toktamish, rather than Abraham, Levi or Jacob? Clearly not: this Toktamish was a Tartar, a converted Nogäi or the son of a convert.[36]

The conversion of the Khazar kingdom is of great importance for the question of the origins of the Jews who lived in the Danubian lands and southern Russia. These regions contain large Jewish populations, who are probably in no way, or almost no way, ethnographically Jewish. A particular circumstance must have brought into Judaism many people who were not Jews by race. This was slavery or household servitude. We can see how in

35   It is hard to believe that Renan could be mistaken, but Amharic is a Semitic language, and the Bible was translated into Ge'ez.
36   The Nogaïs were a people of a fundamentally Turkic language, established in the Caucasus; they were descendants of the Kipchaks.

all the Christian countries, but especially the Slavic lands, the great preoccupation of the bishops and councils was to prohibit Jews from having Christian servants. Household service favoured proselytism, and the slaves of Jews very often end up professing Judaism themselves.

It is beyond doubt, therefore, that Judaism initially represented the tradition of a particular race. It is also beyond doubt that the phenomenon of the formation of the present Jewish race includes a contribution of original Palestinian blood; but, at the same time, I am convinced that there is in the Jewish population as a whole, as it exists today, a large share of non-Semitic blood; so much so that this race, which is viewed as the ideal of a pure ethnos, preserving itself across the centuries by the prohibition of mixed marriages, has been strongly permeated by foreign infusions, much as has been the case with all other races. In other words, Judaism was originally a national religion; it has become in our own day a closed religion; but in the interval, over long centuries, Judaism had been open; large masses of non-Israelite populations embraced Judaism; so that the meaning of this word, from the ethnographic point of view, has become very dubious.

People will raise against me the objection of what is called the Jewish type. A great deal might be said on this point. My opinion is that there is no one Jewish type, though there are indeed Jewish types. I have gained much experience in this respect, from having been associated for ten years with the Bibliothèque Nationale's collection of Hebrew manuscripts, so that Jewish scholars from around the world addressed themselves to me in order to consult our valuable collection. I very soon came to recognize my clients, and from the far end of the room I could tell those who were on the way to my office. Well, the result of my experience is that there is not a single Jewish type, but that there are rather several such types, who are absolutely irreducible to one another. How did a race manage to confine itself, as it were, to a certain number of types? Following from what we said just now, by sequestration, the ghetto, and the prohibition of mixed marriages.

Ethnography is a very obscure science, since it is impossible to carry out experiments, and there is no certainty that it ever will be possible. What I am going to say is not with the object of proof, but simply to explain my thinking. I believe that, if one took a few thousand people at random, for example those walking at this moment along the Boulevard Saint-Germain, and imagined them transported to a desert island and free to multiply; I believe, then, that after a certain time the types would be reduced, massed together in a certain sense, concentrated into a certain number of types that had prevailed over others, which would have persisted and constituted themselves in an irreducible fashion. The concentration of types follows from the fact of marriage being confined for many centuries within a restricted circle.

Another fact adduced in support of the ethnic unity of the Jews is the similarity of customs and habits. Whenever you put people of any race together, and constrain them to a ghetto life, you will have the same results. There is what one might call a psychology of religious minorities, and this psychology is independent of race. The position of the Protestants, in countries like France where Protestantism is a minority, has a strong analogy to that of the Jews, since for a very long time the Protestants were obliged to live in their own community and many things were forbidden them, as with the Jews. Similarities are thus created that do not arise from race, but are rather the result of certain analogies of situation. The habits of a concentrated and confined life, constrained by prohibitions and more or less sequestered, are everywhere the same, regardless of race. The widespread slanders against Protestants and Jews among the more unenlightened parts of the population are the same. The professions that a sect excluded from the common life is compelled to adopt are likewise the same. Like the Jews, Protestants are not a people and do not have a country; they have been prevented from having this.[37] As for mental similarity within the same sect, this is sufficiently explained by the similarity of education, reading and religious practices.

---

37   Research on the Jews of France in the first half of the Middle Ages, as found in volume 27 of the *Histoire littéraire de la France*, shows how, until the decrees of Phillipe le Bel, they followed the same trades and professions as other French people [Renan's note].

In Syria one can observe a fact that supports my present thesis. There are in a dozen places north of Damascus villages where the ancient Syriac language is still spoken, which has almost completely disappeared elsewhere and which is now found only here and much further north, around Van and Ourmia. The people of these villages are Muslim, and resemble all Syrian Muslims as far as their customs are concerned. The differences between Muslims and Christians in Syria are as great as can be imagined: the Christian is the most timid creature, while the Muslim is accustomed to bearing arms and dominating. One would say, at first glance, that there is a very marked ethnographic difference. In relation to the disturbances that occurred in Beirut a few months ago, my distinguished friend, Dr S., wrote me that his housekeeper came home and told him: 'A Muslim child with a sword could have killed a thousand Christians.' And it is here that the situation of these villages around Damascus is so interesting. If there are any authentic Syrians in the world, it is these people here, since they still speak their old language; and yet they are Muslims and resemble all other Muslims in their habits and customs. The difference that exists between them and the Syrian Christians thus results from a difference in their way of life, and a social position that has continued over centuries; it has absolutely nothing to do with ethnography.

In the same way, among the Jews, the particular physiognomy and habits of life are certainly far more the result of the social necessities that have weighed on them for centuries than they are a racial phenomenon.

Let us rejoice, gentlemen, that these questions, which are so interesting for history and ethnography, have no practical importance in France. We have in fact resolved the political difficulty associated with them in the proper fashion. Where nationality is concerned, we make the question of race a completely secondary fact, and we are right to do so. The ethnographic fact, which was capital in the early stages of history, continues to lose its importance to the extent that civilization advances. When the National Assembly decreed the emancipation of the Jews, in 1791, it was extremely little concerned about race. It held that men should be judged not by the blood flowing in their veins, but rather by their moral and intellectual value. It is the glory of France to have dealt with these questions from the human side. The task of the nineteenth century is to break down all ghettos, and I do not respect those elsewhere who seek to raise these again. The Israelite race has rendered the world the greatest services. Assimilated to different nations, in harmony with diverse national units, it will continue to do in the future what it has done in the past. By its collaboration with all the liberal forces of Europe, it will make an eminent contribution to the social progress of humanity.

Printed in the United States
by Baker & Taylor Publisher Services